SINGER®

The New machine quilting essentials

Updated and Revised Edition

Creative Publishing
international

First published in the United States of America by
Creative Publishing international, Inc., a member of
Quayside Publishing Group
400 First Avenue North
Suite 300
Minneapolis, MN 55401
1-800-328-3895
www.creativepub.com

10 9 8 7 6 5 4 3 2 1

Library of Congress Cataloging-in-Publication Data

The new machine quilting essentials. -- Updated and rev. ed.
    p. cm.
  At head of title: Branded by Singer.
  Rev. ed. of: New quilting by machine, c1999.
  Includes index.
  Summary: "Includes basic techniques for quilting by machine, with instructions for piecing different block patterns. Full instructions for 20 projects"--Provided by publisher.
  ISBN-13: 978-1-58923-570-0 (soft cover)
  ISBN-10: 1-58923-570-3 (soft cover)
  1. Patchwork. 2. Machine quilting. I. Singer Company. II. New quilting by machine.

TT835.N472 2010
746.46--dc22

2010023565

Cover Design: Lois Stanfield
Page Layout: Kathleen Littfin

Printed in China

SINGER®

The New machine quilting essentials

Updated and Revised Edition

Creative Publishing
international

CONTENTS

Introduction to Quilting

A quilt is a bed covering, providing warmth, but it is also much more. A quilt holds memories and expresses dreams. It can be a remembrance, an accomplishment, or a record of a shared experience. Designing and making a quilt is a creative outlet, a channel for artistic expression, and a skilled craft. Many quilts are made, not for providing warmth, but for the challenge and pleasure of creating colorful, textural artwork from fabric scraps.

A Brief History

Machine quilting started in the late 1850s and early 1860s when the sewing machine was widely produced. It is estimated that 50 to 75 percent of the quilts made between 1860 and 1940 were machine-stitched. All-white quilts were popular because their unbroken surface allowed sewing machine owners to show off the capabilities of their new machines. In the mid-twentieth century, quilting became less popular, but in the 1970s, largely as a result of the US Bicentennial, quilting became prominent again. The first American National Quilt Show was held in 1979, allowing quilters an opportunity to exhibit and share their latest designs and techniques. Quick-cutting and quick-piecing methods inspired people to take up quilting. Machine quilting was rediscovered, allowing quilters to do more in less time. Now machine quilting is a favorite pastime of millions of women and men who value their craft as an outlet for creative expression and leisure-time enjoyment.

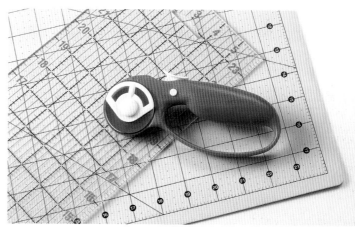

How to Use This Book

New Machine Quilting Essentials can be used as a learning tool if you are sewing your first quilt or as a reference if you have quilting experience. The piecing, appliqué, and quilting techniques that are included in this book are quick, easy machine methods. While helping you make more efficient use of your time, these methods also increase accuracy and durability.

The Quilt Designs section shows various block designs that are built on basic geometric shapes. It also shows how the arrangement of the blocks, color choices, and color placement will affect the overall look of the quilt. Tips for color and print selection will guide you to design success.

The Getting Started section helps you determine quilt size and calculate the yardage needed for quilt tops and backs. There is information to help you select fabrics, batting, notions, and equipment, as well as suggestions for setting up your work area.

The Quilt Tops section teaches quick techniques for cutting various shapes and for piecing or appliquéing a dozen traditional block designs. Plain and decorative sashing and border ideas are taught so you can choose the one that enhances your pieced design.

The Quilting section provides information on marking, assembling, and basting the quilt. You will learn three different quilting techniques and three methods of binding a quilt. Information on caring for, storing, and displaying quilts is also included. Complete directions for creating each project shown in the Quilt Tops section are provided at the end of the book.

There are many traditional quilt designs, and some have more than one name. Not all quilt designs are included in this book, but with the information on drafting quilt blocks, you will be able to copy other quilts or create designs of your own. With The New Machine Quilting Essentials as your guide, you can enjoy a lifetime of machine quilting pleasure.

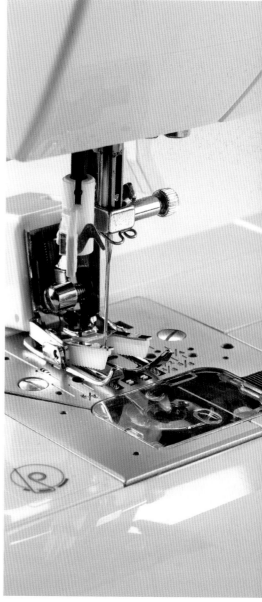

A Quilter's Vocabulary

Become acquainted with the terms that are used to describe the methods and materials for quilting. You will find these words throughout the book, and you will also hear them spoken in your local quilt shop.

Acid-free materials. Paper products, including tissue paper, cardboard tubes, and boxes, made especially for the storage of textiles. They do not contain the chemicals, normally found in wood and paper products, that can weaken and destroy fabric over time.

Appliqué. A cut fabric shape stitched to another piece of fabric.

Backing. Fabric used for the bottom layer of a quilt.

Batting. The middle layer of a quilt, which provides loft and warmth.

Bias. The diagonal of a piece of fabric. A true bias is at a 45-degree angle to both the lengthwise and crosswise grainlines of the fabric. The greatest amount of stretch in a woven fabric is on the true bias.

Binding. The strip of fabric used to enclose the edges of the three layers of a quilt.

Block. A square unit, usually made up of pieces of fabric sewn together in a design. Blocks are combined to make a quilt top.

Borders. Strips of fabric forming a frame around the quilt top. Borders may be plain or pieced.

Chainstitching. Sewing seams of several fabric pieces without breaking the stitching between the pieces. Also called chaining.

Fat quarter. A half-yard (0.5 m) of fabric, cut down the middle to measure 18" × 22" (46 × 56 cm). This is the equivalent of a quarter-yard (0.25 m) of fabric.

Free motion quilting. See freehand quilting.

Freehand quilting. Guiding the quilt through the sewing machine by using your hands, rather than pressure from the feed dogs and presser foot. Also called free motion quilting.

Lattice. See sashing.

Loft. The thickness and springiness of the batting.

Machine-guided quilting. Guiding the quilt through the sewing machine using pressure from the feed dogs and presser foot.

Medallion quilt. Quilt top with a central motif, usually framed by multiple borders.

Miter. To join corners at a 45-degree angle.

Piecing. Stitching together pieces of fabric to create a larger unit.

Quilt. A bedcover or wall hanging made by stitching together a top fabric, batting, and backing fabric.

Quilting. Stitching through a top fabric, a batting layer, and a backing fabric in a design to add texture and to hold layers together.

Sampler quilt. A pieced quilt made up of many different block designs, rather than a single, repeated block design.

Sashing. Strips of fabric, plain or pieced, that divide the blocks in a quilt. Also called lattice.

Set. The way blocks are positioned in a quilt. They may be arranged in straight or diagonal rows.

Strip-piecing. Creating pieced designs from long strips of fabric by stitching the strips together, cutting them crosswise, and then stitching the pieces together to form a design.

Template. A pattern made of plastic or cardboard, used to trace cutting or stitching lines onto fabric.

Template-free. A method for cutting pieces using a ruler, instead of a template, as a guide.

Tied quilt. A quilt that is held together with ribbon or yarn, rather than with quilting stitches.

Anatomy of a Quilt

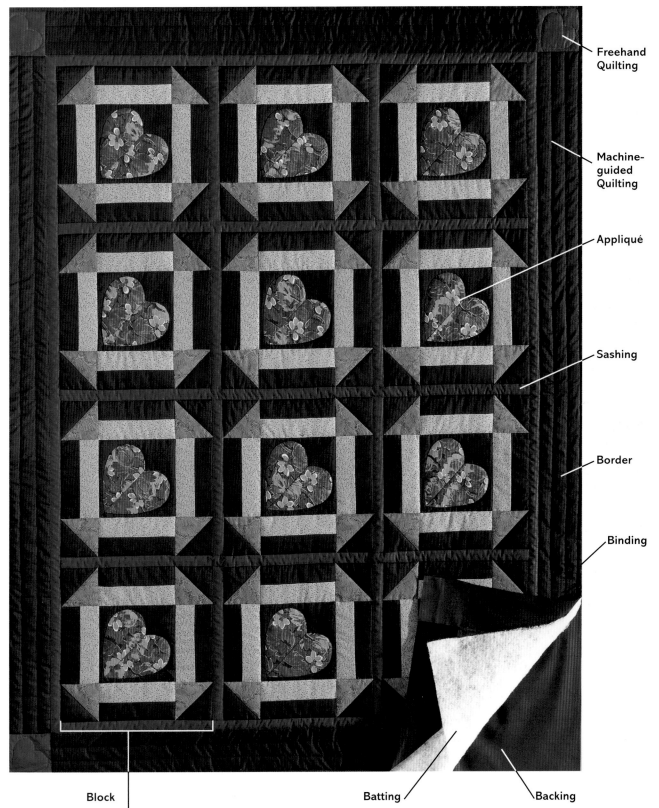

Freehand Quilting

Machine-guided Quilting

Appliqué

Sashing

Border

Binding

Block

Batting

Backing

Table runner

Selecting a
Quilting Project

Start small and keep choices simple. Before making a full-size bed quilt, you may want to sew a smaller project that can be completed quickly, such as a pillow, table runner, or doll quilt. Before making a decision, it may be helpful to look through the entire book for more ideas.

You may want to experiment with several piecing techniques, using a different technique for each project. Or you can make a sampler quilt, using a different design for each block. You can also choose one block design for the entire quilt, varying the color and fabric.

Doll quilt

Pillows

Once you have decided on a project, you will need to make several other decisions, such as design, color, whether or not you want sashing or borders, and what type of binding you will use. It is not necessary to make all these decisions before you start your project, but it is helpful to have a basic plan in mind.

Choose template-free patterns. Template-free designs allow you to cut multiple pieces at one time and often allow you to use quick-piecing techniques. Designs that require templates must be traced individually onto fabric. They take more time to cut and are usually more difficult to assemble. Most of the patterns included in this book are template-free. Patterns are arranged in order, from designs that are easy to sew to those that are more difficult.

Placemats and wall hanging

Wall hanging

Crib quilt

11

QUILT DESIGNS

Selecting a Design

Many quilters use a traditional quilt design rather than creating their own. This simplifies the design process. Study designs made by other quilters in order to see the effects of color, fabric, setting, and border variation.

Take your time selecting a design. Look at as many quilts, or photos of quilts, as possible. Quilt shops are a valuable source for design ideas. They generally carry an extensive selection of books and magazines and often have quilts on display.

Or, you may prefer to create your own design, rather than follow instructions from a book or magazine.

Shapes

Most piecing designs for quilt blocks are made up of one or more geometric shapes, such as squares, rectangles, triangles, and diamonds. Designs made up of curved shapes are less common, because they require more time and skill to construct. The more intricate curved shapes are usually appliquéd.

Block Designs

The most common type of quilt top is made up of blocks. A block is a pieced square of fabric. The number of squares that make a block can be four, nine, sixteen, twenty-five, or more. The pieces in a the block may be identical, as in Patience Corner (page 14), which is made up of nine square pieces of fabric. Or they may be varied, as in Ohio Star (page 16), with triangles and squares creating the block, or Churn Dash (page 16), which is made up of squares, rectangles, and triangles. Some block designs, such as Log Cabin (page 14), do not divide into smaller squares.

The possible combinations for making blocks are infinite. Several different block designs can be stitched together to create a sampler quilt. But most quilt tops use a pattern of repeating blocks. The blocks may be arranged in many ways, called settings (pages 18 and 19), which can vary the overall quilt design.

Block Designs with Squares

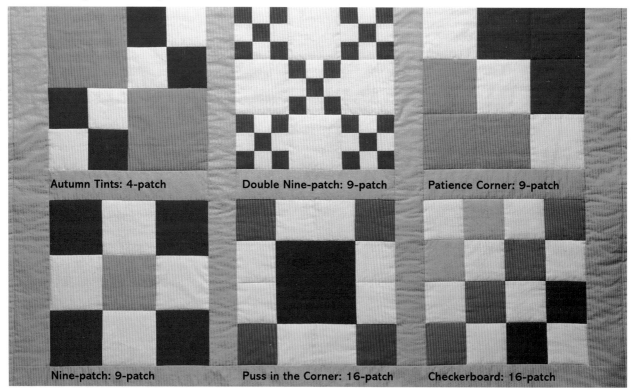

Autumn Tints: 4-patch

Double Nine-patch: 9-patch

Patience Corner: 9-patch

Nine-patch: 9-patch

Puss in the Corner: 16-patch

Checkerboard: 16-patch

Block Designs with Rectangles

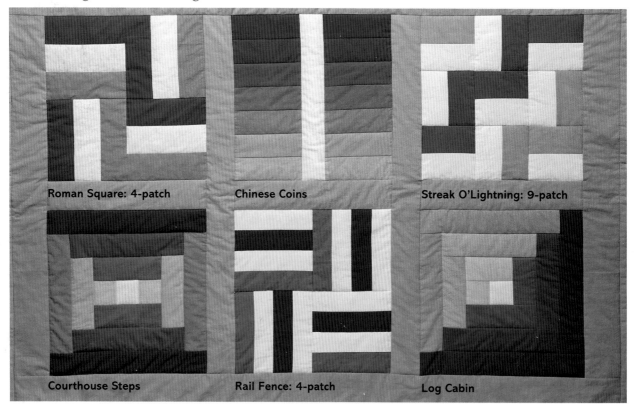

Roman Square: 4-patch

Chinese Coins

Streak O'Lightning: 9-patch

Courthouse Steps

Rail Fence: 4-patch

Log Cabin

Block Designs with Triangles

Yankee Puzzle: 4-patch

Card Trick: 9-patch

Birds in Air: 9-patch

Dutchman's Puzzle: 16-patch

Brown Goose: 16-patch

Lady of the Lake: 25-patch

Block Designs with Curves

Lafayette Orange Peel: 4-patch

Wheel of Fortune: 4-patch

Robbing Peter to Pay Paul: 16-patch

Queen's Crown: 16-patch

Wonder of the World: 16-patch

Vine of Friendship: 25-patch

Block Designs with a Combination of Shapes

Bright Hopes: 4-patch

Churn Dash: 9-patch

Rolling Stone: 9-patch

Ohio Star: 9-patch

Puzzle Boxes: 9-patch

Maple Leaf: 9-patch

Clay's Choice: 16-patch

Evening Star: 16-patch

Road to Oklahoma: 16-patch

Grandmother's Choice: 25-patch

Cake Stand: 25-patch

Crown of Thorns: 25-patch

Quilt Designs without Blocks

Block designs are the most common designs, but there are many that cannot be broken down into blocks. One-patch quilts are made up of pieces that are all the same shape and size. Any shape can be used for a one-patch quilt.

Medallion quilts have a central motif that can be pieced, appliquéd, or quilted. The motif is then surrounded by multiple borders. Many of these quilt designs require a template and specific piecing instructions.

Trip Around the World is a one-patch quilt made up of squares.

Thousand Pyramids is a one-patch quilt made up of triangles.

Carpenter's Wheel is a medallion quilt with a central motif surrounded by a larger motif.

Lone Star is a medallion quilt with a single central motif made up of small diamonds.

Settings for Quilts

Blocks may be arranged in a number of ways, which are called settings, or sets. Changing the setting can make the same block design look different.

When pieced blocks are placed side by side, design lines, such as squares or diagonals, may become evident. Placing sashing strips between blocks or alternating plain and pieced blocks can produce two entirely different looks. You can also place the blocks on their points, either with or without sashing. When designing a quilt, you may want to try a variety of settings, using many photocopies of the block design or the actual pieced blocks to determine the setting you like best.

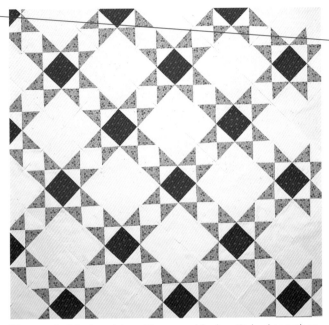

Diagonal side-by-side settings are blocks stitched together in diagonal rows, so that blocks stand on their points. Often, a diagonal setting creates a sense of motion or appears to add curves to a pieced design.

Side-by-side settings are commonly used. Individual blocks are stitched together in rows. This makes the blocks blend together and may reveal an overall pattern.

Straight alternating block settings use pieced blocks alternating with plain blocks. The plain blocks reduce the amount of piecing required and provide space for freehand quilting stitches.

Diagonal alternating block settings are the same as straight alternating block settings, except the blocks are turned on their points.

Straight sashing settings have strips of fabric between side-by-side blocks. This defines the individual blocks and provides a framework that unifies different block designs.

Diagonal sashing settings are the same as straight sashing settings, except the blocks are turned on their points.

Copying a Quilt Design

To copy a quilt design, isolate one block by finding where the design starts to repeat itself in each direction. Look at the entire quilt to see if all the blocks are the same; some quilts have two or more different block designs. When a quilt includes more than one design, it is necessary to draft each design separately. Quilts with blocks on a diagonal will also have half or quarter blocks to complete the quilt top.

Look at each quilt block to see how many squares it is divided into. Draw the block on a plain piece of paper or quilter's graph paper. Divide this block into squares, and then divide it again into smaller shapes. It is easier to copy blocks made up of squares, rectangles, or triangles; most diamonds and curved shapes require templates.

Identifying the Block Design

Examples of quilt designs include those made up of two or more block designs (left), one-block designs set on the diagonal with sashing (middle), or one-block designs set side by side (right). Each block breaks down into squares, rectangles, triangles, or a combination of shapes. Copy each different block design, opposite.

How to Draft a Quilt Block

1 Visualize a grid of equal squares on quilt block. The block may be divided into four, nine, sixteen, or more equal squares.

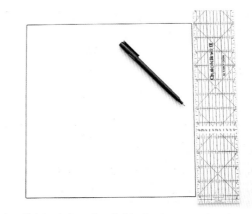

2 Determine finished size of quilt block; choose a size that divides easily, such as 6", 9", or 12" (15, 23, or 30.5 cm) for a 9-patch block, or 8" or 12" (20.5 or 30.5 cm) for a 16-patch block. Draw a square on paper the size of finished block.

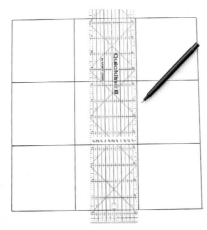

3 Divide each side of the square by the number of squares on each side of quilt block; mark grid.

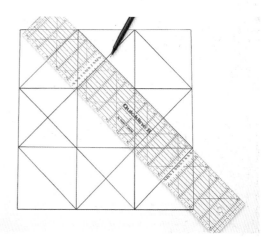

4 Determine the smaller shapes that make up each square of the quilt block; draw corresponding horizontal, vertical, and diagonal lines.

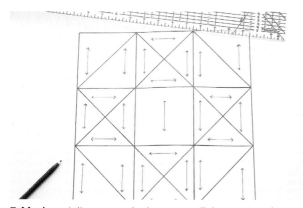

5 Mark grainline on each shape, parallel to outer edges, to use as a reference when cutting.

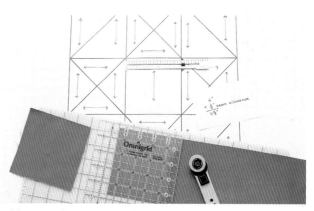

6 Measure finished size of each shape; cut pieces, adding seam allowances (pages 54 and 63).

Designing a Quilt Block

Create your own designs by starting with basic shapes, such as right triangles, squares, or rectangles; or use a combination of shapes. Shade in some of the shapes you selected, using only black, white, and gray; the design will stand out, and you will not be distracted by colors or fabrics.

Then make many photocopies of these basic shapes. Cut them out and arrange them in various combinations to create a block. Next, arrange several blocks until you can see the overall quilt design, so you can tell if diagonals or zigzags are created. Sashing may be added between blocks, if desired. This process gives you an infinite number of design possibilities.

How to Design a Quilt Block

1 Start with a square made up of right triangles or any other shapes. Shade some of the shapes and make photocopies; cut them out.

2 Arrange four squares in various ways to create four-patch quilt blocks; tape in place. Make photocopies of these blocks; cut them out.

3 Arrange four blocks in various ways to create 16-patch blocks; tape in place. Make photocopies; cut them out.

4 Continue, trying various arrangements, until you create the design you like or the size you need.

Borders for Quilts

A border is a fabric frame that surrounds a quilt. The color chosen for the border can highlight different designs and fabrics within the quilt. A quilt may have a single border or multiple borders of varied widths. Interrupted or pieced borders add interest and can repeat a design in the quilt or sashing.

Four Borders for Quilts

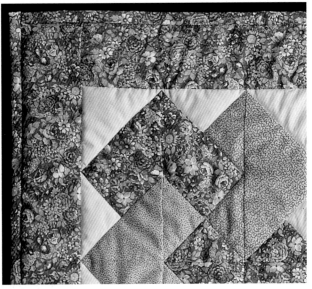

Single border is a fabric strip of any width, stitched to the edges of the pieced design.

Multiple border is made of two or more borders of varied widths.

Interrupted border is broken by a small plain or pieced block, usually at the corners. A checkerboard unit (page 57) is frequently used.

Pieced border is made of randomly spaced pieces (shown) or of pieced strips, such as Flying Geese strips (page 65).

Selecting Colors

A traditional design can be made to look contemporary by the choice of color. Choosing different colors can transform the design from soft to bold or from soothing to vibrant. The placement of solid colors or prints can change the look of a design, emphasizing the individual blocks, or diagonal, vertical, or horizontal lines.

Color selection is a matter of personal preference, but because there are so many color choices available, making a decision may be difficult. It is helpful to look at existing quilts or pictures of quilts. You can choose the color combination of any quilt design and use it for the design you have chosen. Another source of help is a quilt shop, where quilting experts can offer suggestions.

When selecting colors, look for combinations of light, medium, and dark. Contrasting or intense colors can help emphasize parts of a design. Combine prints close in color value to create a blended look. Vary the size of the prints to add interest. Add variety to a quilt by using different prints or colors in each block. When you shop for fabric, stack the bolts you have selected; then step back and squint at them. This helps you see which colors stand out and which colors may be too similar. It also gives you a clear idea of the overall color and whether the prints are too close in scale. Substitute bolts of fabric until you are satisfied. If you want the quilt to coordinate with your decorating scheme, bring samples of paint, wallpaper, or drapery or upholstery fabric when selecting fabric for the quilt.

Use the color wheel as a guide and choose prints and solids in different color values.

Choose a printed fabric and select two or three colors from the print for the solid colors in the quilt.

Color Selection & Placement

The same block design can have an entirely different look depending on what colors are used and how they are placed. An endless variety of combinations is possible. Experiment with color placement, using fabric swatches or colored pencils on photocopies of the same quilt design, to discover totally different effects.

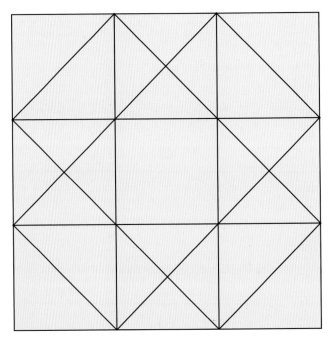

Cut shapes from fabric swatches and glue or tape them to a sketch of the design. Or use colored pencils to experiment with color combinations.

Use basic color schemes to help with color selection, such as shades of one color **(1)**, similar or related colors **(2)**, opposite or complementary colors **(3)**, and multiple colors **(4)**.

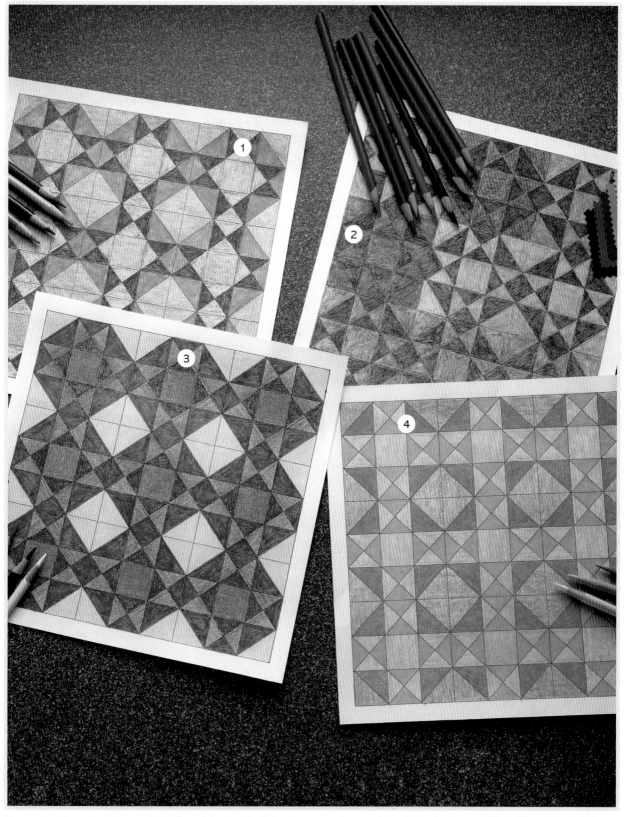

Use color placement to create different looks. Similar colors may be used in all blocks for a unified effect **(1)**. A different color in each block will set them apart **(2)**. By changing color placement, the same design can highlight diamonds **(3)** or squares **(4)**.

Tips for Color and Print Selection

Combine print fabrics and solid-colored fabrics. Use bleached or unbleached muslin for background pieces.

Use contrasting colors in each block.

Choose compatible color combinations, usually warm (top) or cool (bottom). Use combinations of light, medium, and dark colors.

Stack bolts of fabric you are considering on a table, step back, and squint. Buy ¼ yd. (0.25 m) of each fabric selected and make a few test blocks.

Use different prints in similar colors in each block. Distribute dominant prints and colors evenly throughout the quilt.

Combine large-scale and small-scale prints.

GETTING STARTED

Determining the Finished Size

The first thing you must know in order to figure yardage requirements is the finished size of the quilt. If you are making the quilt for a bed, the finished size is determined either by the measurements of the bed or by the size of the packaged batting. If you are making the quilt to hang in a particular space, you can measure the space available.

To determine the finished size of a quilt by the bed measurements, measure the bed with the blankets, sheets, and pillows that will be used with the quilt. If you are using a thick batting, place the batting on the bed along with the bedding to ensure that the quilt will be large enough.

Measure the width of the bed from side to side across the top; do not include the pillows. Then measure the length of the bed from the head of the bed to the foot; if the quilt is to include a pillow tuck, include the pillow in the length measurement, tucking the tape around and under the pillow as you plan to tuck the finished quilt. A pillow tuck usually adds an additional 10" to 20" (25.5 to 51 cm) to the length, depending on the size and fullness of the pillows.

For the drop length, measure from the top of the bed to the desired length. For a comforter, measure to just below the mattress, about 9" to 12" (23 to 30.5 cm) down from the top of the bed. For a coverlet, measure to just below the box spring, about 18" (46 cm) down from the top of the bed. For a bedspread, measure to the floor, about 20½" (52.3 cm) down from the top of the bed. Add two times the drop length to the width of the bed for the two sides, and a single drop length to the length of the bed for the foot.

Determine the finished quilt size by the packaged batting sizes (page 41). Batting should be 2" to 4" (5 to 10 cm) larger on each side than the finished quilt. Packaged battings are usually sized for coverlets.

Adjust the finished measurements of the quilt according to the thickness of the batting and the amount of quilting you plan to do. For most average-size quilts with low or medium-loft batting, shrinkage due to quilting is about 2 to 3 percent. For high-loft batting, shrinkage may be 5 to 6 percent.

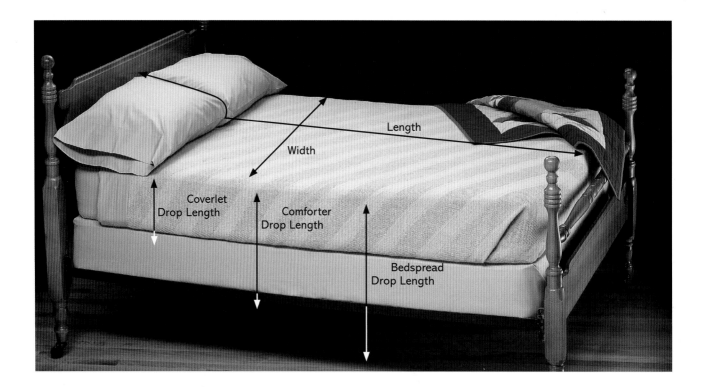

Adjusting the Quilt Size

There are several ways to alter a design to fit the specific measurements of the quilt. Change the size of the sashing strips, borders, or blocks. Or change the number of borders or blocks.

It is easier to change the size of the sashing strips and borders than the size of pieced blocks. The relationship between sashing strips, borders, and blocks should remain in proportion. For most quilts, a combination of methods is used to adjust the size.

Four Ways to Adjust the Quilt Size

Increase or decrease the width of the sashing strips or borders.

Increase or decrease the number of borders.

Increase or decrease the number of blocks in the lengthwise or crosswise rows.

Increase or decrease the size of the blocks.

Calculating Yardages

Determine yardage for a quilt either by calculating the yardage exactly or by making an estimate. If you are estimating yardage, you will need to buy extra fabric to ensure that you have enough to complete the entire design.

To estimate yardage, a comforter-length pieced quilt top for a full-size bed will require a total of 10 to 12 yards (9.15 to 11.04 m) of fabric. Divide this amount proportionately by the number of fabrics in the design. To calculate yardage exactly, sketch the outline on graph paper and indicate the different fabrics and shapes by coloring or shading. Mark the measurements and scale clearly on the sketch. Calculate yardages for one fabric at a time, starting with the largest and longest pieces. As you work through the yardage calculations, sketch the cutting layout for each fabric. Working from the largest to the smallest pieces

ensures the most economical use of fabric, particularly if the borders are cut lengthwise. Allow for some shrinkage and do not include selvages when calculating yardage. If the fabric is to be preshrunk, plan for about 40" (102 cm) of usable width on the cutting layouts for 45" (115 cm) fabric.

How to Calculate Yardage for Sashing

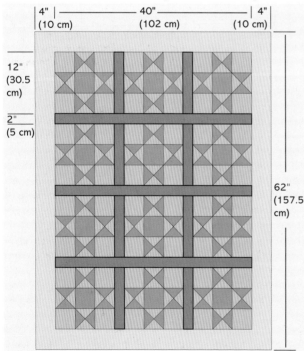

1 Use sketch of quilt top, labeled with measurements of blocks, borders, and sashing strips; draw seams for sashing on sketch.

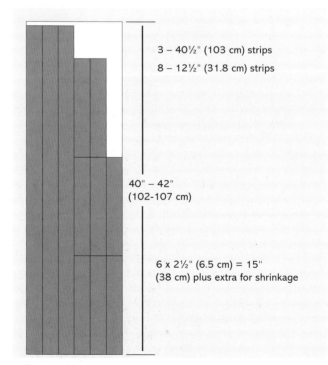

3 – 40½" (103 cm) strips
8 – 12½" (31.8 cm) strips

40" – 42" (102-107 cm)

6 x 2½" (6.5 cm) = 15" (38 cm) plus extra for shrinkage

2 Draw cutting layout for sashing strips, labeling usable width of fabric. Sketch sashing strips, including seam allowances, on crosswise or lengthwise grainline, as desired, labeling measurements. Add measurements on length of sketch to determine yardage.

Binding

To determine the yardage for ½" (1.3 cm) binding, measure the outer edges of the quilt and add the measurements together. Divide this number by 40" (102 cm), the usable fabric width, and multiply by 3" (7.5 cm), the cut width of the binding.

Sashing

When sketching the quilt and drawing the cutting layouts for sashing, keep in mind that the short sashing strips are used between the quilt blocks in each row. If the sashing is cut on the crosswise grainline, three short sashing strips can usually be cut across the width of the fabric. Long sashing strips are used between the rows. If the sashing is cut on the crosswise grainline, it may be necessary to piece the long sashing strips. The seam placement is usually planned so the seams fall in the center of each long sashing strip.

Borders

Borders are usually the largest pieces in a quilt top. They can be cut from a continuous length of fabric, or they can be pieced. Except for small quilts, continuous borders will have to be cut on the lengthwise grainline. They usually require more total yardage than pieced borders. When piecing borders, plan the placement of seams or let them fall randomly around the edges. Randomly placed seams should not be closer than 12" (30.5 cm) from a corner. Seams may be stitched straight across the width of the fabric or on the bias.

Blocks

Blocks contain the smallest pieces of fabric in a quilt. Calculate the yardage for each fabric separately. If blocks are cut from the same fabric as the sashing, borders, or bindings, the yardage for the blocks should be calculated last, because the remaining fabric may not be the full width.

How to Calculate Yardage for Borders

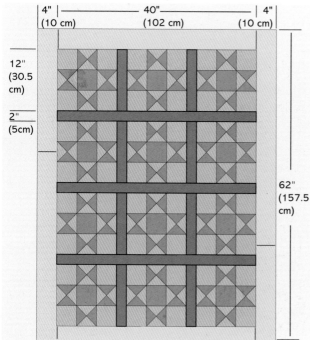

1 Use sketch or quilt top, labeled with measurements of blocks, borders, and sashing strips. Plan placement of border seams, if desired; draw seams on sketch.

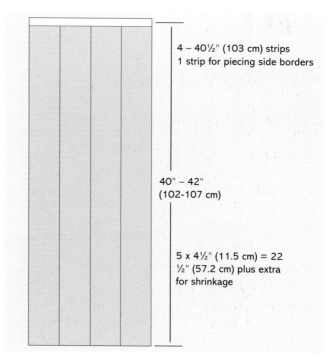

2 Draw cutting layout for borders, labeling usable width of fabric. Sketch border strips, including seam allowances, on crosswise or lengthwise grainline, as desired, labeling measurements. Add measurements on length of sketch to determine yardage.

How to Calculate Yardage for Quilt Blocks

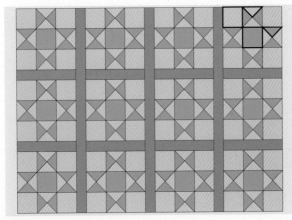

Pink
12 – 4½" (11.5 cm) squares
96 triangles (cut from 5¼"
[13.2 cm] squares)

Yellow
48 – 4½" (11.5 cm) squares
96 triangles (cut from 5¼" [13.2 cm]
squares)

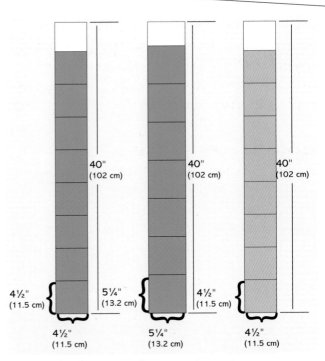

1 Determine number of individual shapes of each fabric needed for quilt top. Refer to cutting instructions (pages 50, 54, 63, and 69) for cutting shapes from strips.

2 Determine how many shapes can be cut from one crosswise strip, using about 40" (102 cm) as usable width of most fabrics, or remaining width, if sashing, borders, or binding have been cut from same fabric.

4½" (11.5 cm) Pink Squares

Number shapes needed	12
Divide by number shapes per strip	÷ 8
Equals number strips to cut	= 1½
(Round up to next whole number)	2

Pink Triangles (cut from 5¼" [13.2 cm] squares)

Number shapes needed	96
Divide by number shapes per strip	÷ 28
Equals number strips to cut	= 3⁀₇
(Round up to next whole number)	4

4½" (11.5 cm) Yellow Squares

Number shapes needed	48
Divide by number shapes per strip	÷ 8
Equals number strips to cut	= 6

Yellow Triangles (cut from 5¼" [13.2 cm] squares)

Number shapes needed	96
Divide by number shapes per strip	÷ 28
Equals number strips to cut	= 3⁀₇
(Round up to next whole number)	4

4½" (11.5 cm) Pink Squares

Width of strip	4½" (11.5 cm)
Times number of strips	× 2
	= 9" (23 cm)

Pink Triangles (cut from 5¼" [13.2 cm] squares)

Width of strip	5¼" (13.2 cm)
Times number of strips	× 4
	= 21" (53.5 cm)

4½" (11.5 cm) Yellow Squares

Width of strip	4½" (11.5 cm)
Times number of strips	× 6
	= 27" (68.5 cm)

Yellow triangles (cut from 5¼" [13.2 cm] squares)

Width of strip	5¼" (13.2 cm)
Times number of strips	× 4
	= 21" (53.5 cm)

Pink	Yellow
9" (23 cm)	27" (68.5 cm)
+ 21" (53.5 cm)	+ 21" (53.5 cm)
= 30" (76 cm)	= 48" (122 cm)

Plus ¼ yd. (0.25 m) each

3 Divide number of shapes needed by number that can be cut from strip; round fractions up to nearest whole number. This is the number of strips to be cut.

4 Multiply number of strips times width of each strip to determine yardage needed. Add ¼ to ½ yd. (0.25 to 0.5 m) for shrinkage and testing design.

Backing Fabric

Yardage for backing fabric is based on the quilt top measurements and whether or not the backing will be seamed. Backing fabrics should extend 2" to 4" (5 to 10 cm) beyond the edges of the quilt top on all sides to allow for shrinkage during quilting.

Some fabrics are available in 90" and 108" (229 and 274.5 cm) widths, but most are 45" (115 cm) wide and will have to be seamed (page 101). It is helpful to make a sketch of the quilt back, including seams, to calculate yardage. This information below is for 45" (115 cm) fabric with a usable width of about 40" (102 cm).

Crib quilts usually do not require seaming because they can be made from one width of backing fabric cut to the desired length. For crib quilts, allow only 1" to 2" (2.5 to 5 cm) on all sides for shrinkage during quilting.

How to Calculate Yardage for Backing Fabric

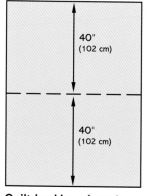

Quilt backings for twin-size quilts less than 80" (203.5 cm) long can be pieced horizontally for the best use of fabric.

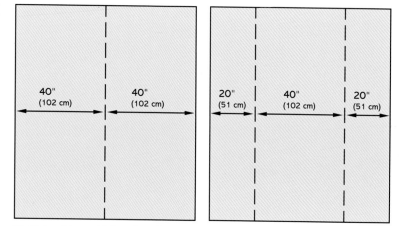

Quilt backings 40" to 80" (102 to 203.5 cm) wide require seaming two widths of fabric together. The two widths can be seamed down the center of the quilt, or one of the widths can be cut and seamed to the sides.

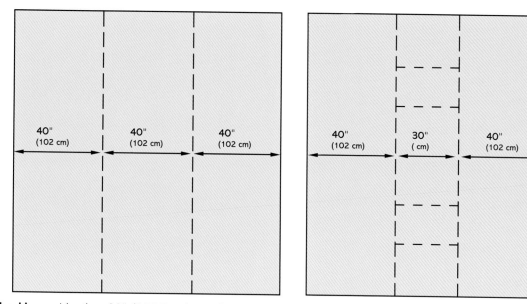

Quilt backings wider than 80" (203.5 cm) usually require three widths of fabric seamed together. Or use two widths of fabric at the sides and piece a center panel from matching or contrasting fabrics.

Selecting Fabrics

Fabric is usually selected after a quilt design and color scheme have been chosen, although a special piece of fabric may help create a design idea or establish color for a quilt. Many kinds of fabric can be used for a quilt, but a primary consideration is fiber content.

Fabric of 100 percent cotton is the best choice for quilts. Cotton fabric is easy to cut, sew, and mark; it is also easy to press, holds a crease well, and is available in a wide range of colors and prints. The quality and weight of cotton fabric is determined by thread count. The thread count is the number of threads per inch (2.5 cm) of fabric. In high-quality cotton fabric, the thread count is equal lengthwise and crosswise; this is called an even weave. Most quilting cottons are either 78-square or 68-square. Fabrics with lower thread counts are too lightweight.

Cotton/polyester blends resist wrinkling and abrasion, making them a suitable choice for frequently washed quilts. The different lengthwise and crosswise thread counts in cotton/polyester blends cause a different amount of stretch along the lengthwise and crosswise grains, which can make it more difficult to piece fabrics accurately. Also, when stitched, cotton/polyester blends tend to pucker more than 100 percent cotton fabrics.

Choose good-quality fabrics that are compatible with the function of your quilt. If you are making a comforter for a child's bed, the quilt will be subject to hard and constant use; select fabrics that can withstand wear and frequent washing. If you are making a wall hanging, the durability of the fabric is less important.

Types of Quilting Fabrics

Quilting fabrics include prints, tone-on-tones, solids, broadcloths, hand-dyed fabrics, flannels, backing fabrics, and muslin.

Prints can include calicos, country prints, novelty prints, and designer-inspired prints. Tone-on-tones are used for backgrounds and transitions in your quilt design.

Solids and broadcloths come in every color including black and white. Kona brand is readily available.

Hand-dyed fabrics are 100 percent cotton and are available in gradations of color and other designs. Hand-dyed fabrics give your quilt a unique look. These fabrics can be purchased at some quilting stores, quilting shows, and from mail-order sources.

Flannel suitable for quilting is available at some quilt stores. It is especially nice for children's quilts. It also makes a cozy backing for your quilt.

Muslin is a utility fabric used for foundation bases. It is generally a lighter weave and comes in a variety of widths.

Selecting Backing Fabrics

Select a backing fabric that has the same care requirements as the fabrics in the quilt top. Fabrics of 100 percent cotton are the best choice for machine quilting, because they do not pucker as much as cotton/polyester blends. Some fabrics are manufactured specifically for quilt backing. They are 100 percent cotton and are available in 90" and 108" (229 and 274.5 cm)

widths, so they usually do not require piecing. These fabrics are available in light-colored prints on white backgrounds and a few solid colors. If the quilt will be finished with a mock binding (pages 120 and 121), choose a backing fabric that will coordinate with the quilt top. If you want to showcase the quilting stitches, use a solid. Printed fabrics tend to hide the stitches.

Tips for Selecting Backing Fabrics

Solid-colored fabric accentuates the quilting stitches; printed fabric tends to hide the stitches.

Backing fabric should not show through to the quilt top when the batting has been sandwiched between the layers. If it does show through, change to a lighter-colored backing fabric.

Preparing the Fabric

If you plan to wash the quilt, test dark or vivid-colored fabrics for colorfastness to determine whether the dye bleeds to light-colored fabrics or colors the water. If colors do bleed, repeat the test; if a fabric still bleeds, it is probably not colorfast.

Fabrics can be preshrunk by machine-washing them using a mild soap, such as dishwashing soap. Do not use soap intended for fine woolens; it may yellow cotton fabrics. Machine-dry the fabric, using a warm setting.

Preshrinking fabrics removes excess dyes and chemical finishes used in the manufacturing process. Most cotton fabrics shrink 2 to 3 percent when washed and dried, so if they are not preshrunk, the fabrics may pucker at the stitching lines and the finished size of the quilt may change the first time it is washed. After preshrinking, you may want to press the fabric, using spray starch, to make cutting and stitching easier.

Fabric is not always woven with the threads crossing at 90° angles; however, it is usually not necessary to straighten the grainline. Minor variations in the grainline do not change the overall look of a quilt block and straightening the grainline may waste as much as 4" (10 cm) of a piece of fabric.

How to Test Fabric for Colorfastness

1 Fill jar or glass with warm water and a few drops of mild soap, such as dishwashing soap.

2 Cut 2" to 6" (5 to 15 cm) square of fabric. Place in water. Allow to soak until the water has cooled slightly. Swish fabric.

3 Place wet fabric on sample of light-colored fabric for the quilt; blot dry. If dye transfers to light-colored fabric, repeat the test; if fabric still bleeds, it is probably not colorfast.

Selecting Batting

Batting is the middle layer of a quilt. The loft, or thickness, of the batting determines the warmth or springiness of the quilt. Batting is purchased according to the amount of loft desired (opposite). The most widely used fibers for batting are cotton and polyester, or a blend of the two (referred to as 80/20). Cotton batting gives a flat, traditional appearance when quilted. Polyester batting gives a puffy look and is more stable and easier to handle than cotton batting. Cotton/polyester batting combines the flat appearance of cotton with the stability and ease in handling of polyester. New fiber blends are now available including bamboo and silk. Fusible batting eliminates the need for hand basting. It is useful for smaller lap quilts. Your quilt shop can advise you on the benefits of each type of batting.

Two types of batting are frequently used: bonded and needlepunch. Bonded batting is made by layering fibers and then adding a finish to hold the fibers together and make the batting easier to handle. Needlepunch batting is made by layering the fibers and then passing them through a needling machine to give a dense, low-loft batting. It is firm, easy to handle, and warm. Most needlepunch batting is polyester. The minimum distance between quilting stitches varies from one batting type to another and is noted on the batting package.

The fibers in batting may migrate, or move, affecting the appearance of the quilt. Bonded batting is treated to help control fiber migration. There are two forms of fiber migration: bunching and bearding. Bunching is the migration of fibers within a quilt, causing thick and thin areas. Bunching can be controlled by placing the quilting stitches ½" to 1" (1.3 to 2.5 cm) apart. Bearding is the migration of fibers through the surface of the quilt. Polyester batting tends to beard, and these fibers may pill. Cotton batting may beard, but the fibers break off at the surface. To help prevent bearding, use a closely woven fabric for the quilt top and backing. Black batting is the best choice for a

dark colored quilt. If bearding does occur, clip the fibers close to the surface of the quilt: do not pull the batting through the fabric. After clipping the fibers, pull the quilt top away from the batting so the fibers return to the inside of the quilt.

Batting is available in a wide range of sizes, although the selection in certain fibers and construction types may be limited. Polyester batting has the widest range of sizes and lofts. Batting should extend 2" to 4" (5 to 10 cm) beyond the edges of the quilt top on all sides to allow for the shrinkage that occurs during quilting. Batting is packaged for standard-size quilts. It is also available by the yard and in smaller packages for clothing and craft projects.

Guidelines for Selecting Batting

Fiber Content	Appearance of Finished Quilt	Characteristics	Spacing of Quilting Stitches
Cotton	Flat	Absorbs moisture, cool in summer and warm in winter	½" to 1" (1.3 to 2.5 cm)
Polyester	Puffy	Warmth and loft without weight, nonallergenic, moth and mildew-resistant	3" to 5" (7.5 to 12.5 cm)
Cotton/polyester blend	Moderately flat	Combines characteristics of cotton and polyester	2" to 4" (5 to 10 cm)

Batting Thickness

Low-loft	⅛" to ⅜" (3 mm to 1cm)
Medium-loft	½" to ¾" (1.3 to 2 cm)
High-loft	1" to 2" (2.5 to 5 cm)
Extra-high-loft	2" to 3" (5 to 7.5 cm)

Packaged Batting Sizes

Crib	45"x 60" (115 x 152.5 cm)
Twin	72"x 90" (183 x 229 cm)
Full	81"x 96" (206 x 244 cm)
Queen	90"x 108" (229 x 274.5 cm)
King	120"x 120" (305 x 305 cm)

Tips for Selecting Batting

Low-loft bonded cotton or cotton/polyester batting is easiest to handle.

Medium-loft adds texture to the finished quilt. The higher the loft, the more difficult to machine-quilt.

High-loft and extra-high-loft battings are best used for tied quilts because they are difficult to machine-quilt.

Notions & Equipment

A few carefully selected notions can make quilting easier and help improve your accuracy in cutting, marking, and sewing.

Quilting can be done entirely on a straight-stitch conventional sewing machine. Choosing the correct type of sewing machine accessories, such as presser feet and needle plates, can help improve your results.

Measuring & Cutting Tools

See-through rulers (1) serve as both a measuring tool and a straightedge for cutting with a rotary cutter.

Measurements are visible through the ruler, so you can cut without marking. Many sizes and types of see-through rulers are available. A ruler 6"× 24" (15 × 61 cm) is recommended, because it is versatile.

Features of rulers vary widely. Some rulers are printed with measurements in two colors to show clearly on both light and dark fabrics. Some have a lip on one edge to hook onto the edge of the cutting mat for easier alignment. Some are printed on the underside to prevent distortion and increase accuracy; if the lines and numbers are molded on the underside, it will help prevent slippage. Square rulers, and rulers with 30°, 45°,

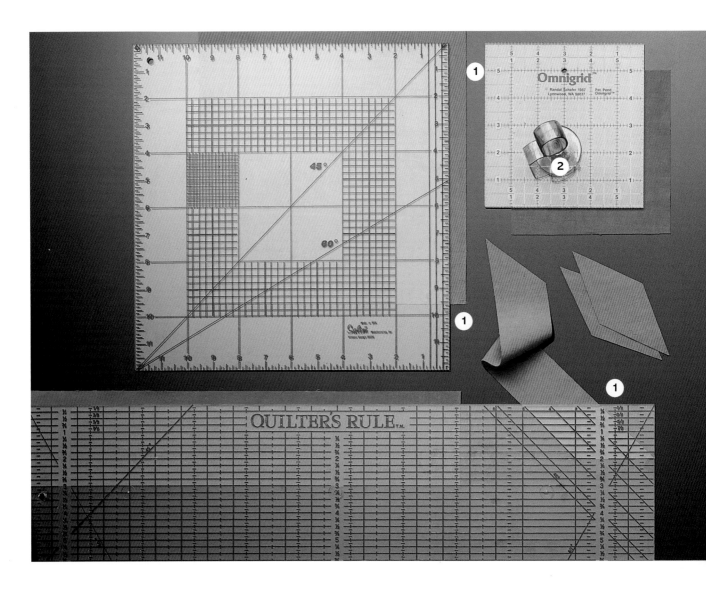

and 60° angle lines, are available. Choose rulers that have the features most important for the type of quilting you are planning to do.

Suction rings (2) and **suction handles** (3) are available to help in positioning a ruler.

Rotary cutters (4) allow you to cut smooth edges on multiple layers of fabric quickly and easily. The cutters are available in various sizes: the smaller size works well for cutting curves or a few layers of fabric; the larger sizes work well for cutting long, straight edges or many layers of fabric.

Cutting mats (5), made especially for use with rotary cutters, protect the blades and the table. They may be plain, or printed with a grid and diagonal lines. A mat printed with a grid is helpful for cutting right angles. Mats come in a variety of sizes. Choose a mat at least 22" (56 cm) wide to accommodate a width of fabric folded in half.

Sewing scissors (6) and **shears** (7) are used for cutting shapes and clipping threads. **Craft knives** (8) are used for cutting cardboard, paper, and plastic templates for pieced or appliquéd designs.

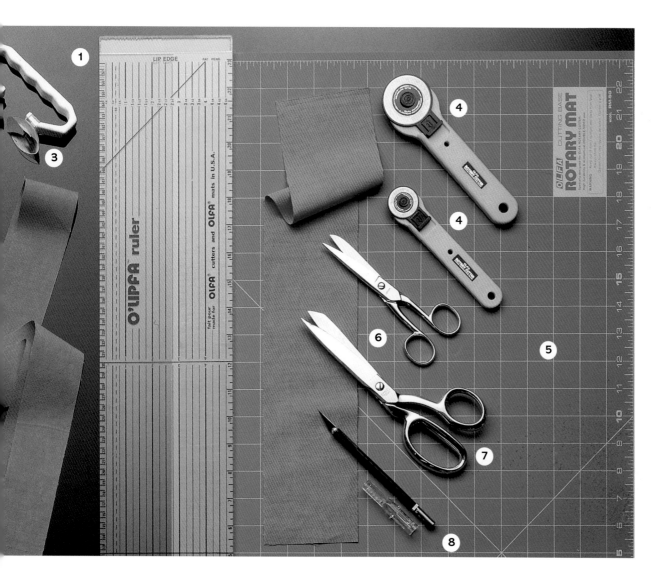

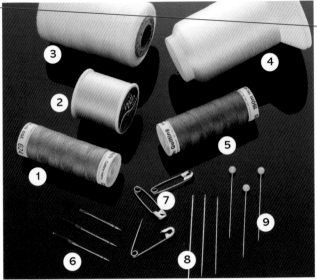

Marking Tools

The markings on a quilt should last only as long as you need them, and you should be able to remove them easily and thoroughly without damaging the quilt. Always test markers on fabrics to see how long the markings last and to be sure they can be removed. Mark lightly; it is more difficult to remove markings that are embedded in the fibers.

A special **fabric eraser (1)** can be used to remove **light lead pencil (2)** marks without abrading or leaving marks on the fabric. **Oil-free and wax-free colored pencils (3)** may also be used for marking. Choose a color close to the fabric color; or choose silver, because it shows on most fabrics. Remove marks before pressing the fabric or washing it in hot water; heat may set pencil marks. **White water-soluble pencils (4)** are available for marking dark fabrics; remove marks with a damp cloth. **Soapstone pencils (5)** are made of pressed talc and marks can be rubbed off or wiped off with water.

Chalk wheels (6) are available in a variety of shapes and colors; marking id fine and accurate. Chalk-wheel marks brush off easily, are washable, and will not stain.

A variety of **plastic sheets (7)** is available for making your own templates. **Precut templates (8)** are available for marking traditional quilting designs.

Sewing & Quilting Tools

For ease in stitching, thread should be of good quality. For piecing, use **100 percent cotton (1)** or **all-purpose sewing thread (2)**; match thread color to the darker fabric or use a neutral color, such as black, cream or gray, to blend. For basting, use a fine, **white cotton basting thread (3)**, or white all-purpose thread; the dye from dark thread could rub off on fabrics.

For quilting, 100 percent cotton thread is usually the best choice. Fine, .004 mm, or size 80 **monofilament nylon thread (4)**, which comes in smoke or clear, is good for quilting and for invisibly stitching appliqués, because it blends with all colors. **Cotton quilting thread (5)** without a finish may be used for machine quilting; however, quilting thread with a special glace finish should not be used for machine quilting. Quilting thread may either match or contrast with the fabric.

Insert a new **sewing machine needle (6)** before beginning a quilting project. For piecing and appliqué, use a size 9/70 or 11/80; for machine quilting, use a size 11/80 or 14/90 needle, depending on the thickness and fiber content of the batting.

Safety pins (7) are essential for pin-basting a quilt; 1" (2.5 cm) rustproof pins work well for most quilting projects. Use **milliners' needles (8)** for thread-basting, because they are long and have small, round eyes. Use glass-head **quilting pins (9)**, because they are long, 1¾" (4.5 cm), and strong.

Sewing Machine Equipment

A straight-stitch conventional sewing machine is used for quilting. The stitch length should be easy to adjust, because you start and end lines of stitches by gradually increasing or decreasing the stitch length.

An entire quilt can be made using only the straight stitch, but several additional features, common on most sewing machines, expand your quilting options. A blind-hem stitch can be used for attaching appliqués. Feed dogs that can be covered or dropped allow you to do freehand quilting.

Presser Feet

Special presser feet are not necessary foe machine quilting, but they can improve your results. For machine-guided quilting, an **Even Feed foot (1)** is recommended for pucker-free stitching. The feed dogs on the Even Feed foot work with the feed dogs of the sewing machine to pull layers of fabric through at the same rate of speed. For freehand quilting, you can either use a **darning foot (2)** or stitch without a foot, depending on the sewing machine.

Use a **general-purpose foot (3)**, or a special-purpose foot for zigzag and blindstitching. A **straight-stitch foot (4)** can improve the quality of stitches, particularly when piecing fabrics with the narrow seam allowances that are standard in quilting.

Needle Plates

Use a **general-purpose needle plate (5)** with the general-purpose or special-purpose foot for zigzag and blindstitching. Use a **straight-stitch needle plate (6)** with the straight-stitch foot for straight and uniform seams and quilting lines. The small hole in the needle plate keeps the fabric from being pushed down into the sewing machine as you stitch. Also use the straight-stitch needle plate with the Even Feed foot for machine-guided quilting and with the darning foot for freehand quilting.

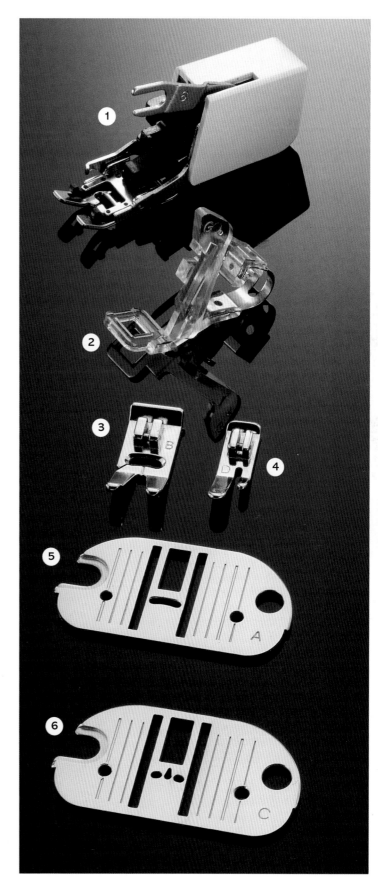

The Work Area

The most important considerations in arranging a work area for machine quilting are comfort and convenience. Be sure the sewing machine is at a comfortable height, so that your shoulders are relaxed when you are quilting. If possible, choose a cutting surface that is approximately hip height. The cutting area should be able to accommodate about one yard (0.95 m) of fabric.

Position the sewing, pressing, and cutting areas so they are convenient to each other; be sure you have a good source of light over each area. Set up the iron and ironing board within easy reach, because seam allowances are pressed frequently during piecing.

A flannel board in a neutral color is valuable when you are designing a quilt. You may use felt or batting instead of flannel. When hanging the flannel board on a wall or door, make sure there is room to step back and view the total design. Use the board when determining how fabrics work together before stitching blocks, when judging the effect of different designs, or when evaluating various settings.

To make quilting easier, expand the sewing surface to support the fabric both to the left of and behind the sewing machine. The surface should be continuous and smooth, so the quilt will move freely, without catching. The surface should be at the same height as the bed of the machine, if possible. If you are using a free-arm sewing machine, convert it to a flatbed.

For a portable sewing machine, place the machine 5" to 6" (12.5 or 15 cm) in from the front edge, and allow enough room to the left of the machine to support the quilt.

For a sewing machine in a cabinet, pull the cabinet away from the wall. Place one table behind it, and another under the leaf, to provide support for the quilt and to reduce strain on the hinges of the cabinet.

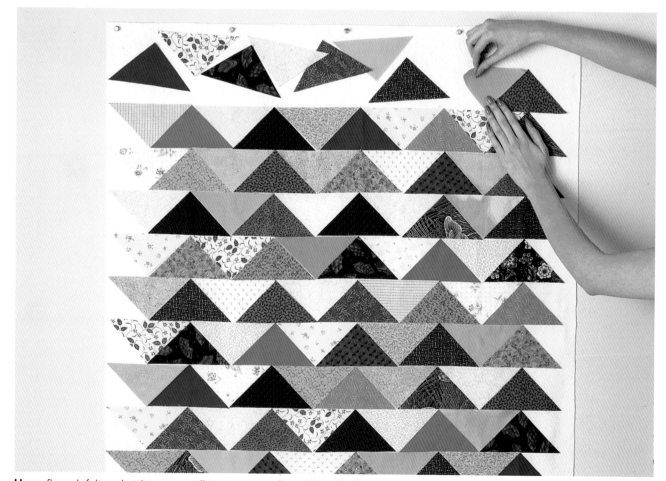

Hang flannel, felt, or batting on a wall to serve as a flannel board when designing a quilt; fabric pieces will adhere without pins.

QUILT TOPS

Basic Piecing Techniques

The designs in this section are for basic, traditional quilt patterns and range from simple squares to more complex curves and appliqués. With the exception of curves and appliqués, the pieces are cut using template-free methods.

The techniques for setting up the sewing machine and for cutting, stitching, and pressing the fabrics are the same for most pieced designs.

Accuracy is critical to successful piecing. A small error can multiply itself many times, resulting in a block or quilt that does not fit together properly. Check the accuracy of your cutting and stitching frequently. You may want to practice cutting and stitching techniques on a small project before using them on a large project.

Cutting Techniques

The quick-cutting techniques that follow are both timesaving and accurate. Instead of cutting each piece of the quilt individually, stack several layers of fabric and cut them into crosswise strips. The pieces are then cut from these strips, eliminating the need for templates.

Determine the grainline by folding the fabric in half and holding it by the selvages. Then shift one side until the fabric hangs straight. It is not necessary to straighten quilting fabrics that are off-grain or to pull threads or tear fabrics to find the grainline.

Good-quality cutting equipment helps ensure that every piece you cut is exactly the right size and that all the pieces fit together perfectly. Use a rotary cutter with a sharp blade and a cutting mat with a printed grid.

Tape three or four thin strips of fine sandpaper across the width of the bottom of a see-through ruler, using double-stick tape. This prevents the ruler from slipping when you are cutting fabric.

How to Cut Fabric Strips

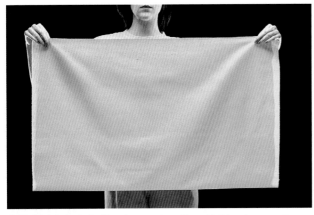

1 Fold fabric in half, selvages together. Hold selvage edges, letting fold hang free. Shift one side of fabric until fold hangs straight. Fold line is straight of grain.

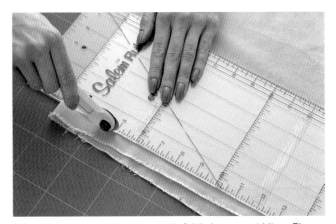

2 Lay fabric on cutting mat, with fold along a grid line. Place ruler on fabric close to raw edge at 90° angle to fold. Trim along edge of ruler, taking care not to move fabric. Hold ruler firmly; apply steady, firm pressure on blade. Stop when rotary cutter gets past hand.

3 Leave blade in position; reposition hand ahead of blade. Hold firmly and continue cutting. Make sure the fabric and ruler do not shift position.

4 Place ruler on fabric, aligning trimmed edge with appropriate measurement on ruler. Hold ruler firmly; cut as in steps 2 and 3. After cutting several strips, check fabric to be sure it is still on-grain, as in step 1.

Stitching Techniques

For pieced quilts, seam allowances are traditionally ¼" (6 mm); stitch accurate seam allowances, so all pieces will fit together exactly. If you have a seam guide on your sewing machine, check the placement of the ¼" (6 mm) mark by stitching on a scrap of fabric. If your machine does not have a seam guide, mark one on the bed of the machine with tape.

Use a stitch length of about 15 stitches per inch (2.5 cm). A shorter stitch length may be necessary for stitching curves and is used for securing stitches at the ends of seams. Adjust thread tensions evenly, so the fabric does not pucker when stitched.

Chainstitching is a timesaving technique for piecing. Seams are stitched without stopping and cutting the threads between them. After all the pieces are stitched together, the connecting threads are clipped and the seams are finger-pressed.

Although some quilters prefer working on one block at a time for the satisfaction of completing a block quickly, it is more efficient to sew an entire quilt top in units. Chainstitch together all the smallest pieces from all the blocks; then combine them to create larger units.

How to Chain and Assemble Pieces

1 Start with smallest pieces; stitch together without backstitching or stopping between pieces, to make a chain of two-piece units. Clip threads between units; finger-press seams.

2 Add more pieces to unit, if necessary for quilt block design, chainstitching them together. Clip threads and finger-press.

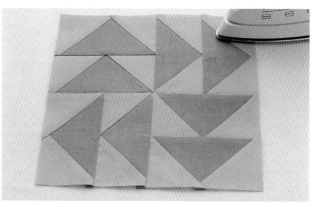

3 Chainstitch units together to create larger units. Clip threads and finger-press.

4 Stitch larger units together to form quilt block. Press with iron.

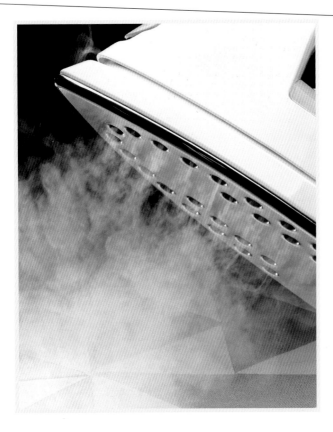

Pressing Techniques

Seams are usually pressed to one side in quilts; however, if you are planning to do stipple quilting (page 119) you may prefer to press the seams open to make it easier to quilt. When pressing seams to one side, it is best to press them to the darker fabric to prevent show-through.

Do not press seams with an iron until a unit or block has straight of grain on all four sides. Always remove all markings from the fabrics before pressing, because the heat from the iron may set marks permanently. When pressing seams, use steam rather than pressure, to prevent the layers from imprinting on the right side. A heavy pressing motion can distort the shape and size of the pieces. Press the blocks first from the wrong side; then press them again lightly from the right side.

The quilt should not be pressed after it is completed because pressing will flatten the batting.

Tips for Pressing

Finger-press individual seam allowances; pressing with an iron can distort bias seams. Press with iron only after a unit or block has straight of grain on all four sides.

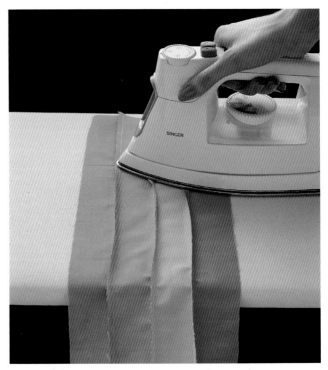

Press long seams with iron by placing strips across, rather than lengthwise on, ironing board, to prevent distorting grainline as you press.

Sewing Designs with Squares

Many quilts are made from nine-patch quilt blocks. A nine-patch block may be made from one-piece squares or pieced squares. A double nine-patch block alternates one-piece squares and checkerboard pieced squares. Each of the checkerboard squares is made from nine smaller squares.

There are two ways to assemble a nine-patch quilt block, the traditional method and the strip-piecing method. The traditional method works well when using larger pieces of fabric, such as 4½" (11.5 cm) squares. The strip-piecing method is used primarily when making quilt blocks with intricate designs, because the piecing can be done quickly without handling small pieces of fabric. A double nine-patch quilt block may be assembled using both the strip-piecing and traditional methods.

The instructions for the nine-patch quilt block (page 55) and the double nine-patch quilt block (page 57) make 12" (30.5 cm) finished blocks.

How to Cut Squares

1 Cut strips of fabric (page 50) the width of one side of square plus ½" (1.3 cm) for seam allowances. Stack three or four strips, matching edges exactly; place ruler on fabric near selvages at 90° angle to long edges of strips. Trim off selvages.

2 Place ruler on fabric, aligning short edge of fabric with appropriate measurement on ruler. Cut to same width as strips, holding ruler firmly.

How to Sew a Nine-patch Quilt Block Using Traditional Piecing

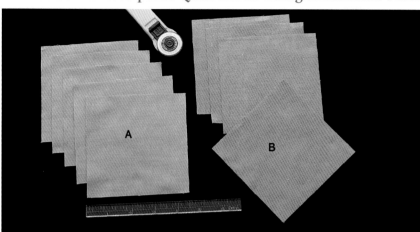

1 Cut five 4½" (11.5 cm) squares from Fabric A. Cut four 4½" (11.5 cm) squares from Fabric B.

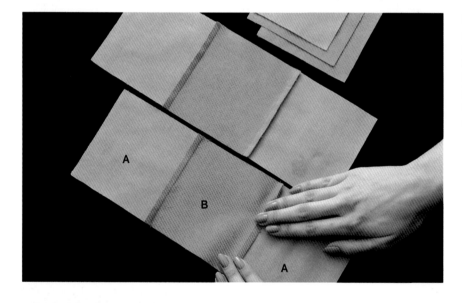

2 Stitch one square of Fabric A and one square of Fabric B, right sides together, using ¼" (6 mm) seam allowances. Stitch another square of Fabric A to other side of Fabric B. . Finger-press seam allowances toward darker fabric. Repeat to make two A-B-A units.

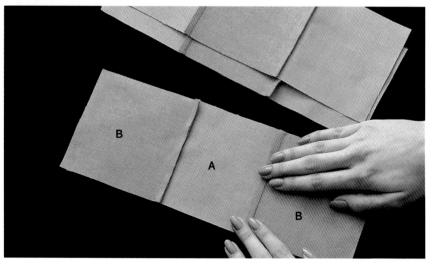

3 Stitch one square of Fabric A and one square of Fabric B, right sides together. Stitch another square of Fabric B to other side of Fabric A. Finger-press seam allowances toward darker fabric.

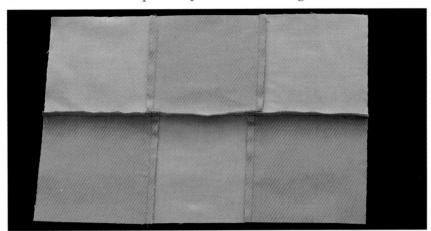

4 Stitch one A-B-A unit to the B-A-B unit, on long edges, right sides together; match seamlines and outside edges, keeping seam allowances toward darker fabric.

5 Stitch remaining A-B-A unit to the other long edge of B-A-B unit, as in step 4.

6 Press long seam allowances to one side; then press from right side.

How to Sew a Double Nine-patch Quilt Block Using Strip-Piecing

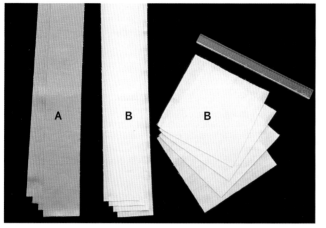

1 Cut two scant 1⅞" (4.7 cm) strips from Fabric A and from Fabric B; cut strips in half to make four 22" (56 cm) strips. Cut four 4½" (11.5 cm) squares from Fabric B.

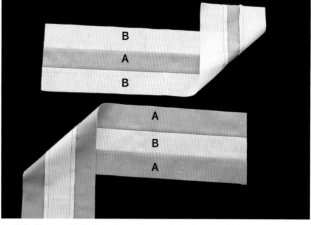

2 Stitch one B-A-B unit and one A-B-A unit, right sides together, using ¼" (6mm) seam allowances. Press seam allowances toward darker fabric.

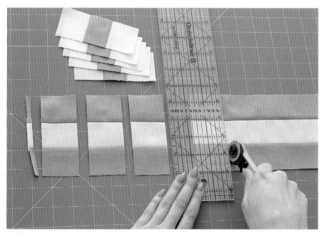

3 Trim short edge of each pieced unit at 90° angle. Cut ten scant 1⅞" (4.7 cm) strips from A-B-A unit. Cut five scant 1⅞" (4.7 cm) strips from B-A-B unit.

4 Stitch one A-B-A unit to one B-A-B unit on long edges, right sides together. Then stitch A-B-A unit to other long edge of B-A-B unit, right sides together, to form checkerboard.

5 Repeat step four for remaining checkerboard units. Press each seam toward side with two darker squares.

6 Stitch checkerboard units and plain units to form a nine-patch quilt block, as in steps 2 to 6, opposite.

Sewing Designs with Rectangles

Rectangles are used in many block designs. Strip-piecing methods are frequently used to piece designs created from rectangles. Streak O' Lightning is one of the easiest of all quilt blocks to strip-piece. Rail Fence uses the same piecing methods, but the strips are narrower.

Log Cabin is one of the most popular and variable traditional designs. Quick-cutting and quick-piecing methods can be used for the Log Cabin block.

Choose fabrics carefully for all three designs, as they define the overall pattern in the quilt top. For example, in the Streak O' Lightning design, choose a light color and a dark color. In the Rail Fence design, where two of the fabrics will define the zigzag pattern on the quilt top, light-to-dark color progressions can be

effective. For the Log Cabin design, three fabrics can be a light color and three a dark color; the center square should be a solid, contrasting, complementary color.

The instructions for Streak O' Lightning and Rail Fence quilt blocks are used when only one quilt block is needed, such as in a sampler quilt or a pillow top. However, when making a quilt top from these designs, it is easier to sew an entire row of squares in a horizontal-vertical-horizontal arrangement the width of the quilt top and then join the rows together.

The instructions for the Streak O' Lightning quilt block (opposite), the Rail Fence quilt block (page 60), and the Log Cabin quilt block (page 61) make a 12" (30.5cm) finished blocks.

How to Make a Streak O' Lightning Quilt Block

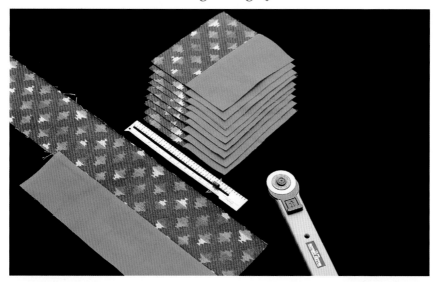

1 Cut one 2½" (6.5cm) strip (page 50) from each of two different fabrics. Stitch strips, right sides together, on long edge. Press seams to one side. Cut nine 4½" (11.5 cm) squares from unit at 90-degree angle to seams.

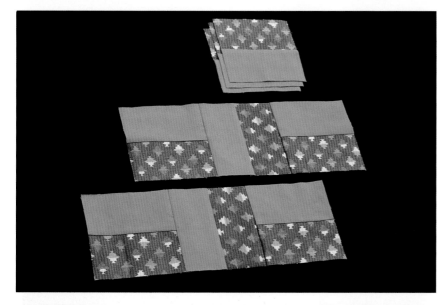

2 Stitch three squares together in a horizontal-vertical-horizontal sequence, as shown. Repeat with three more squares. Keep fabrics in same sequence, from left to right and from top to bottom, throughout quilt. Press seams to same side.

3 Stitch remaining three squares in a vertical-horizontal-vertical sequence. Press seams in opposite direction from other rows. Stitch rows together, with the vertical-horizontal-vertical row in middle. Press seams to one side.

How to Make a Rail Fence Quilt Block

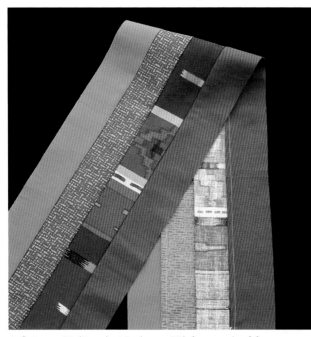

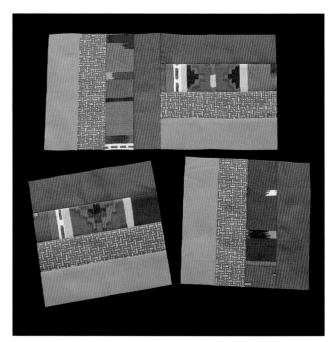

1 Cut one 2" (5 cm) strip (page 50) from each of four different fabrics. When strips are stitched together, outside strips define zigzag pattern. Stitch strips, in sequence, right sides together, along length. Press seam allowances to one side.

2 Cut four 6½" (16.3 cm) squares from unit, at 90-degree angle to seams. Stitch two squares together, in vertical-horizontal arrangement, as shown. Press seam allowances to one side.

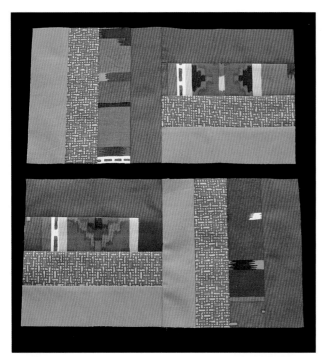

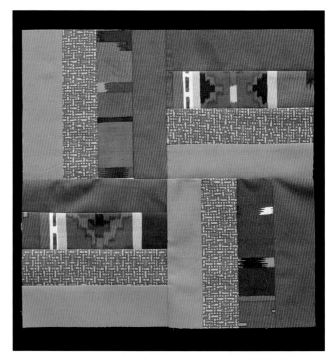

3 Stitch remaining two squares together in horizontal-vertical arrangement, as shown; keep fabrics in same sequence from left to right and from top to bottom throughout quilt. Press seam allowances in opposite direction from first row.

4 Stitch the two rows together, matching seamlines. Press seam allowances to one side.

How to Make a Log Cabin Quilt Block

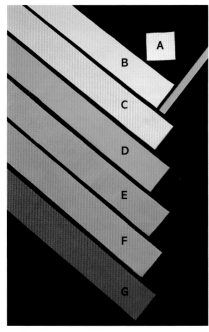

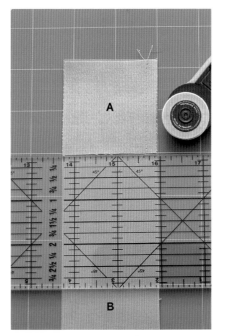

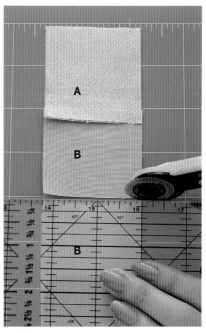

1 Cut one scant 2¼" (6 cm) square from Fabric A. Cut one scant 2¼" (6 cm) strip (page 50) from each of six different fabrics. Label strips from B to G, as shown.

2 Place solid square on Strip B, right sides together. Stitch along one side. Trim stitch even with square. Press seam allowances away from center square.

3 Place pieced unit on remaining length of Strip B, as shown. Stitch on long side. Trim strip even with bottom of pieced unit. Press seam allowance away from center square.

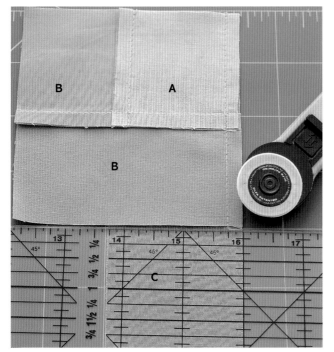

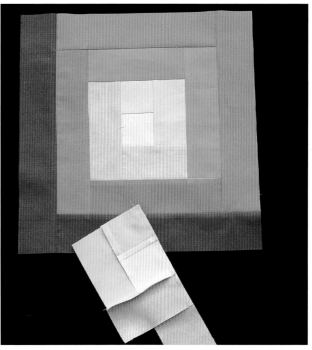

4 Place three-piece unit on Strip C at 90-degree angle to most recent seam. Stitch on long side. Trim strip even with bottom of pieced unit. Press seam allowance away from center square.

5 Place four-piece unit on remaining length of Strip C at 90-degree angle to most recent seam. Continue in this manner, stitching two strips of each color to pieced unit in sequence. Press seam allowances away from center square.

Sewing Designs with Triangles

Triangles are frequently used for quilt blocks. There are two methods for cutting and sewing triangles: the quick-cutting method with traditional piecing and the grid-piecing method.

The quick-cutting method allows you to cut several layers of fabric at one time. Some right triangles are cut with the grainline on the long side and some with the grainline on the short side. The grainline should be on the outside edges of each unit so the edges are stable and will not stretch when units are stitched together. The triangles are then assembled using a traditional piecing method.

The quick-cutting method is used to cut the right triangles for the Flying Geese quilt block (pages 64 and 65); avoid using a fabric with a one-way design. Flying Geese strips may be used for sashing or borders or sewn together to make an entire quilt, as in the crib quilt, below.

The grid-piecing method (page 66) allows you to cut and piece the triangles in one operation. It is used whenever two triangles are stitched together to make a square, commonly referred to as a triangle-square, as in the Pinwheel quilt block (page 67). The grid-piecing method is especially useful when piecing small triangles.

The following instructions for the Flying Geese quilt block (pages 64 and 65) and the Pinwheel quilt block (page 67) make 12" (30.5 cm) finished blocks.

How to Cut Right Triangles Using the Quick-cutting Method

Triangles with short sides on grainline. Cut squares (page 54) with sides the length of finished short side of triangle plus ⅞" (2.2 cm). Cut half as many squares as number of triangles needed. Stack three or four squares, matching edges exactly. Place ruler diagonally across stack, holding ruler firmly; cut.

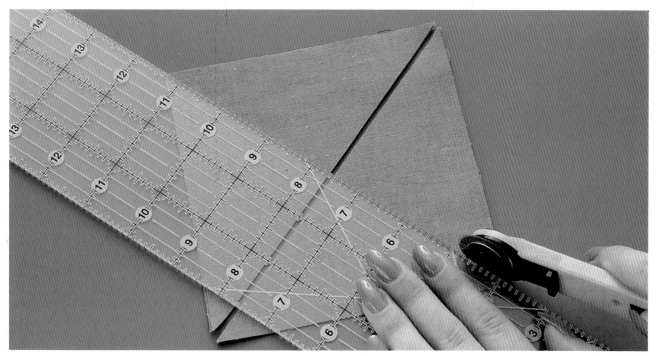

Triangles with long side on grainline. Cut squares (page 54) with sides the length of finished long side of triangle plus 1¼" (3.2 cm). Cut one-fourth as many squares as number of triangles needed. Place ruler diagonally across stack, holding ruler firmly; cut. Place ruler diagonally across stack in other direction; cut.

How to Make a Flying Geese Quilt Block

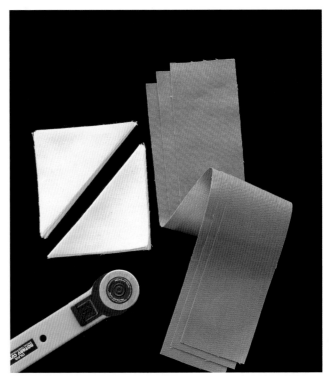

1 Cut three 5¼" (13.1cm) squares of one fabric. Cut through squares diagonally in both directions so long side of each large triangle is on grainline.

2 Cut twelve 2⅞" (7.2 cm) squares of second fabric. Cut through squares diagonally in one direction so short sides of each small triangle are on grainline. Cut three 1⅞" x 12½" (4.7 x 31.8 cm) strips of third fabric.

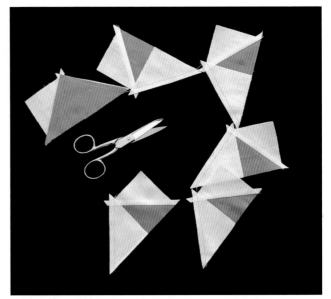

3 Stitch long side of one small triangle to short side of one large triangle, right sides together, using ¼" (6mm) seam allowances and matching corners at base of large triangle; take care not to stretch bias edges. Repeat, using chainstitching, for remaining units; clip apart.

4 Finger-press seam allowances toward small triangle. Stitch a small triangle to other short side of large triangle, right sides together, matching corners at base of large triangle. Take care not to stitch a tuck in first seam. Repeat, using chainstitching, for remaining units; clip apart.

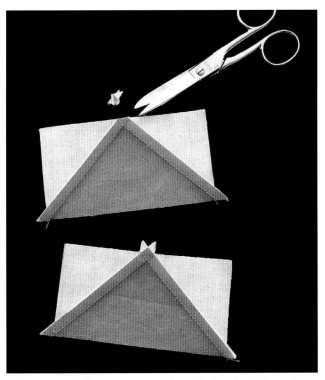

5 Press seam allowances toward small triangles. Trim points.

6 Place two units right sides together, matching top of one unit to bottom of other, so large triangles are pointing in same direction. Stitch, with point of large triangle on top, to make sure stitching goes through point. Repeat, using chainstitching, for remaining units; clip apart.

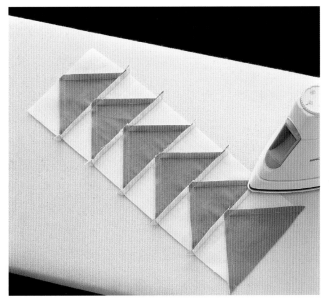

7 Stitch three units together to make a pieced strip of six units. Repeat for a second pieced strip. Press seam allowances toward bases of large triangles.

8 Stitch one long strip between two pieced strips; stitch remaining long strips at sides of block. Press seam allowances toward long strips.

How to Make Triangle-squares Using the Grid-piecing Method

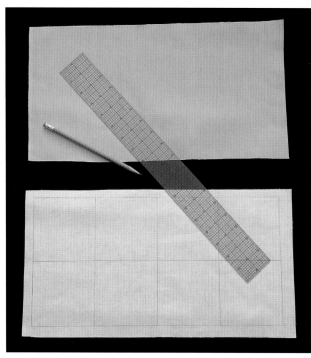

1 Cut one rectangle from each of two different fabrics. Draw grid of squares on wrong side of lighter-colored fabric, making grid squares ⅞" (2.2 cm) larger than finished triangle-square; each square of grid makes two triangle-squares.

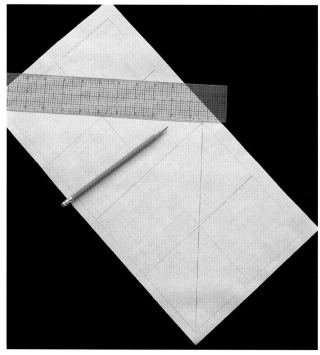

2 Draw diagonal lines through the grid, as shown.

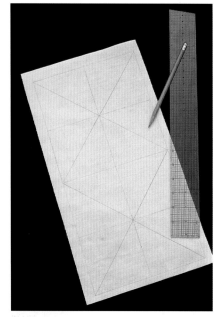

3 Draw diagonal lines through the grid in opposite direction.

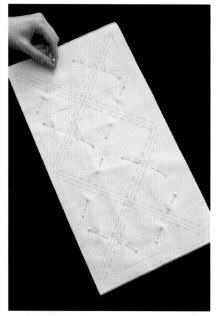

4 Mark dotted stitching lines ¼" (6 mm) on both sides of all diagonal lines. Pin the fabrics, right sides together.

5 Stitch on dotted lines. Cut on all solid lines to make triangle-squares. Press seam allowances toward darker fabric. Trim points.

How to Make a Pinwheel Quilt Block

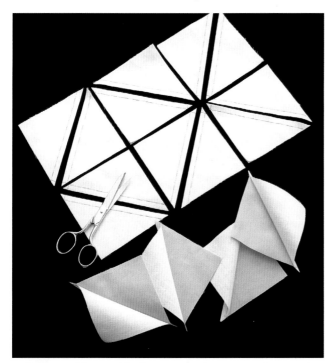

1 Cut one 7¾" × 15½" (20 × 40 cm) rectangle from each of two different fabrics. Draw 3⅞" (9.7 cm) grid, as in step 1, opposite. Draw the diagonal lines, stitch, and cut as in steps 2 to 5, opposite, to make 16 triangle-squares.

2 Stitch two triangle-squares, right sides together, as shown. Repeat with two more triangle-squares. Press seam allowances toward lighter fabric. Stitch two units together to form pinwheel, matching points. Keep seam allowances in alternating directions to eliminate bulk at points. Repeat for three more pinwheels.

3 Stitch two pinwheels together. Repeat with two remaining pinwheels. Press seam allowances in alternating directions.

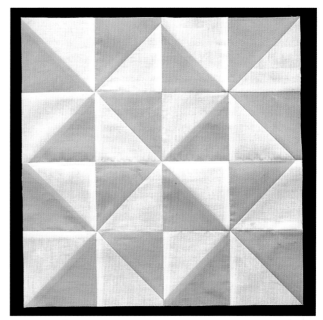

4 Stitch remaining seam to form block. Press seam allowances to one side. Release stitching at centers of pinwheels to make seam allowances lie flat, if necessary, as on page 71, step 10.

Sewing Designs with Diamonds

Diamonds are frequently used to make star designs. Select fabric that has an all-over print or is a solid color rather than fabric with a one-way design or stripes, so you do not have to be concerned about the direction of the design when stitching the pieces together.

Cut diamonds carefully to ensure that the angles are accurate. The cutting directions, opposite, are for diamonds that have 45-degree angles. Other diamond shapes used in quilting require templates for accurate cutting. Because diamonds are cut on the bias, take care not to stretch the edges when stitching.

The instructions for the Eight-pointed Star quilt block (opposite) make a 12" (30.5 cm) finished block.

How to Cut Diamonds

 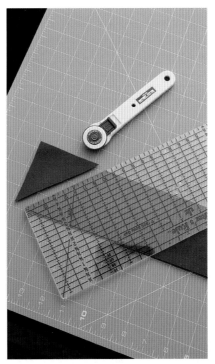 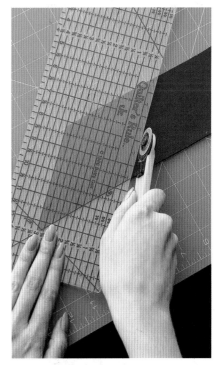

1 Cut strips (page 50) the width of finished diamond plus ½" (1.3 cm). Stack three or four strips, matching edges exactly. Place on cutting mat, along grid line.

2 Place ruler at 45-degree angle to long edge of fabric; hold ruler firmly, and cut.

3 Shift ruler on fabric, aligning fabric edge with measurement mark that is equal to width of strip; hold firmly, and cut. Check accuracy of angle frequently.

How to Make an Eight-pointed Star Quilt Block

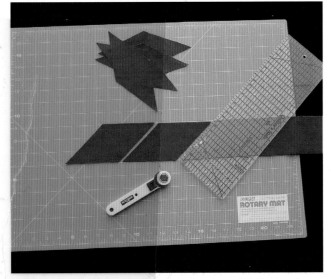 

1 Cut eight 3" (7.5 cm) diamonds from one 3" (7.5 cm) strip of fabric, above, for star.

2 Cut four 4" (10 cm) squares and one 6¼" (15.7 cm) square of background fabric. Cut large square in half diagonally; then cut diagonally in other direction, to make four right triangles.

3 Mark wrong side of quilt pieces where ¼" (6mm) seams will intersect, placing dots at right-angle corner of each triangle, both wide-angle corners of each diamond, and one corner of each square.

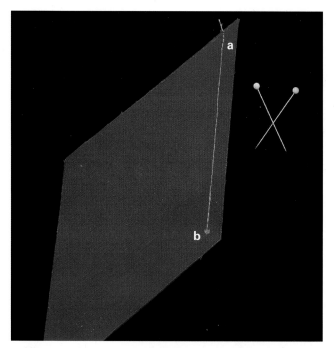

4 Align two diamonds along one side, right sides together, matching inner points **(a)** and dots **(b)**. Stitch from inner point exactly to dot; backstitch. Repeat for remaining diamonds.

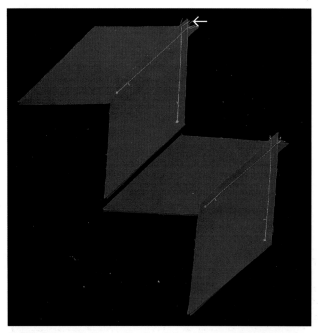

5 Stitch two 2-diamond units, right sides together, as in step 4, folding seam allowances in opposite directions **(arrow)**. Repeat for remaining units.

6 Place two 4-diamond units right sides together. Pin, matching inner points at center. Fold seam allowances of each four-diamond unit in opposite directions to minimize bulk; stitch between dots, securing seams at ends. Do not press.

7 Align short side of triangle to a diamond, right sides together, matching edges at outer point **(a)** and dots at inner point **(b)**. Stitch from outer edge exactly to dot, with diamond side up; backstitch.

8 Align remaining side of triangle to adjoining diamond, and stitch seam as in step 7, with triangle side up. Repeat for remaining triangles, stitching them between every other set of points on the star.

9 Align squares to diamonds between remaining points of star, matching edges at outer point **(a)** and dots at inner point **(b)** stitch with diamond side up, as in step 7. Align the remaining sides of squares and diamonds, stitching with square side up.

10 Release stitching within seam allowances at center of star, so seam allowances will lie flat. Press from wrong side, working from center out.

Sewing Designs with Curves

Some traditional quilt designs are based on curved pieces. Curves are the most difficult shapes to piece, but the more gradual the curve, the easier it is to piece. More intricate curved designs are usually done with appliqué.

Templates are required for cutting curved designs. They are available at quilting stores and by mail order, or you can make your own templates by cutting them from heavy cardboard or plastic template materials. Templates for machine-pieced designs include ¼" (6 mm) seam allowances. Make sure, when tracing and cutting templates, that the edges are smooth and the sizes are exact.

The Drunkard's Path is an easy curved pattern to piece. The pieced squares of the Drunkard's Path can be arranged in many different ways. Three different arrangements are shown, opposite. The method for cutting the templates and fabric for the Drunkard's Path can be use for cutting any machine-pieced curved designs.

The instructions for the Drunkard's Path quilt block (pages 74 and 75) make a 12" (30.5 cm) finished block.

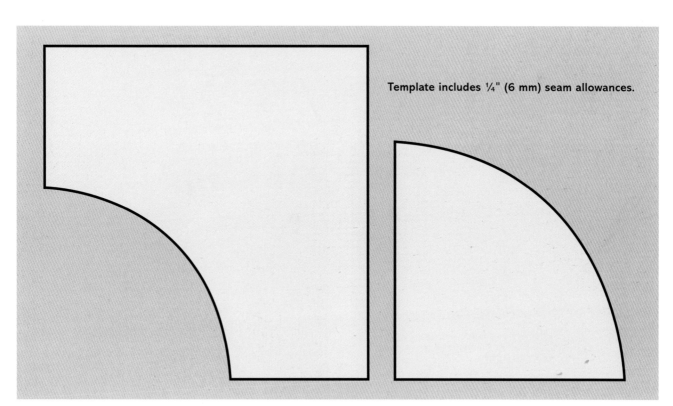

Template includes ¼" (6 mm) seam allowances.

Trace pattern actual size onto tracing paper to make and cut template (page 74).

How to Cut Templates and Fabric for a Drunkard's Path Quilt Block

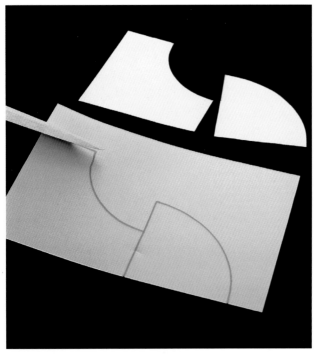

1 Trace template pattern (page 73) accurately onto tracing paper; cut. Place on cardboard or template plastic; trace. Cut accurately.

2 Place large template on one large square, matching edges exactly; trace curve. Repeat for remaining large squares. Cut on marked lines. Discard scraps. Repeat for small squares, using small template.

How to Make a Drunkard's Path Quilt Block

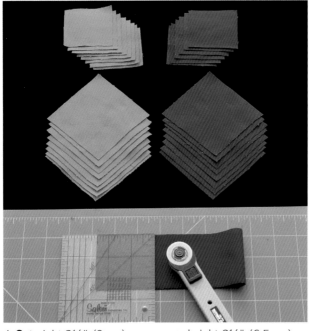

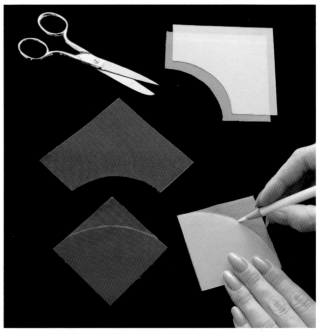

1 Cut eight 3½" (9 cm) squares and eight 2½" (6.5 cm) squares from each of two fabrics.

2 Place template on fabric; trace. Cut fabric on marked line, using scissors or rotary cutter.

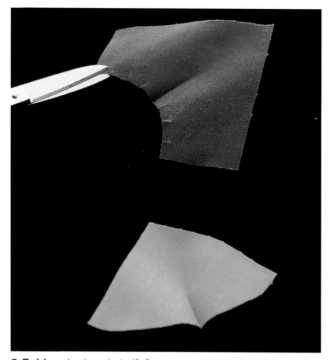

3 Fold each piece in half; finger-press to mark midpoint of curved edge. Clip seam allowances along curves of large pieces ⅜" (1 cm) apart, and a scant ¼" (6 mm) deep.

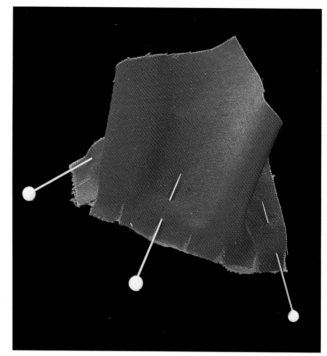

4 Pin one large and one small piece of different fabrics, right sides together, matching center creases. Pin at each corner, aligning edges.

5 Stitch, with large piece on top, lining up raw edges as you sew. Finger-press seam allowance toward large piece. Repeat for remaining pieces.

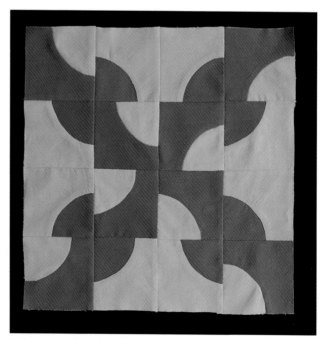

6 Arrange pieced squares in block, four across by four down. First, stitch squares into rows of four; then stitch rows together to complete block. Press.

Sewing Designs with Trapezoids

The Tumbler quilt design is a classic way to use scraps from your fabric stash to make a quilt. Rows of trapezoids, alternating directions, create a lively overall design. The tumblers were traditionally cut using templates to ensure they were all the same size and shape. As long as the top and bottom of the trapezoid are parallel, and the side angles are the same, the scraps fit together in alternating directions to form straight rows. For this modern Tumbler design, a Tri Tool is used to quickly and accurately cut the tumbler patches from fabric strips. Add more rows to create a larger quilt.

The instructions are for a baby quilt that is 45" × 56"(115 × 142 cm).

You Will Need:

¼ yd. (0.25 m) each of ten fabrics for tumblers.

⅝ yd. (0.6 m) for the sashing.

½ yd. (0.5 m) for binding.

Batting, crib size, 45" × 60" (115 × 142 cm)

2½ yds. (2.3 m) for the backing

Tri Rec tool by EZ Quilting

Cutting Directions

Cut two 5" (12.7 cm) strips the width of the fabric from each of the ten fabrics.

Cut eight 2½" (6.4 cm) strips the width of the fabric from the sashing fabric.

Cut six 2½" (6.4 cm) strips the width of the fabric from binding fabric.

How to Cut Trapezoids

1 Place the Tri Tool with the 1½" line on top of strip and the 6½" line along the bottom of the strip. Cut along edges using rotary cutter.

How to Cut Trapezoids (cont.)

2 Flip the Tri Tool around, aligning with freshly cut edge. Reposition yourself or the cutting board to safely cut new edge. Continue cutting pieces, alternating directions. You will get seven tumblers per strip.

How to Make the Tumbler Baby Quilt

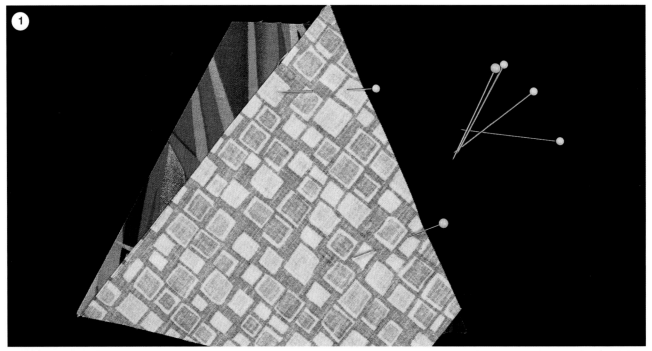

1 Pin two tumbler blocks right sides together, aligning the sides of the tumbler. There will be a ¼" equilateral triangle sticking out at each end. Sew using a ¼" seam allowance. Press and open. Check to see that top and bottom of tumbler are aligned. Repeat, adding tumblers in random order, until you have 18 tumblers in a row.

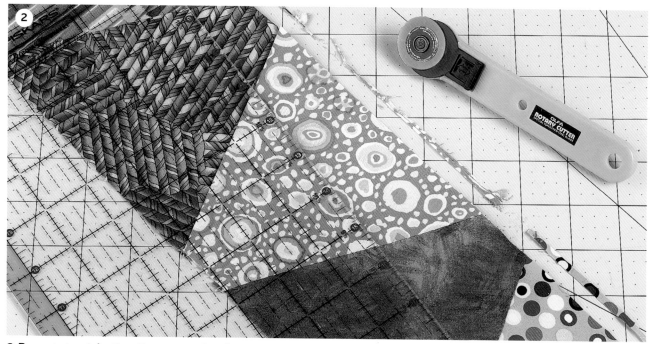

2 Repeat step 1 for the other seven rows. Square the row edges, if necessary.

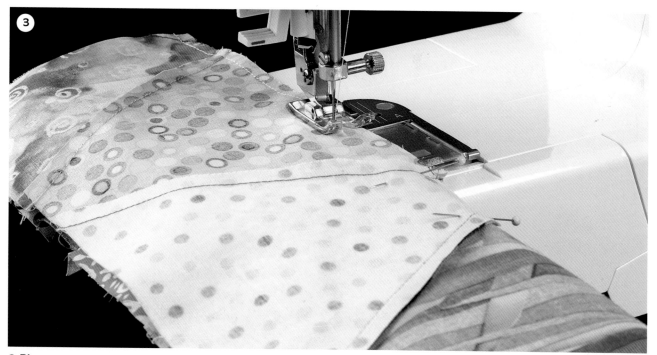

3 Place two rows together to make a mirror image. Pin at intersections, aligning seams. Stitch rows together. Press seam allowances in one direction.

4 Piece sashing to create the needed length. Sew sashing to the 4 mirror image rows and to the outer vertical edges.

5 Cut batting and backing (page 101). Baste layers together. Machine quilt using stitch in the ditch or overall design. Cut and apply binding (page 120).

Sewing Designs with a Combination of Shapes

Often quilt blocks are sewn from a combination of shapes. The shapes can be arranged in the same order in each block, or the overall design might include two or more arrangements of the same shapes.

The Churn Dash pattern is a combination of square, rectangle, and triangle shapes in a nine-patch block. In this traditional quilt pattern, pieced squares form a twisting design around a plain square to imitate the mixing movement of cream against the sides of a butter churn.

Avoid light-colored fabrics for the central design to prevent the background fabric from shadowing at the seamlines. Create an Amish-style quilt, shown on pages 91 and 95, by choosing black fabric for the design and strong solid colors for the various backgrounds. These instructions make a 6" (15 cm) finished block.

The Ohio Star is a nine-patch block made up of squares and triangles. This pillow's block uses three fabrics, but you may also choose to use four different fabrics just for the points of the star (page 90). Select a dominant print for the center square. Choose star point fabrics that are darker or more vibrant than the background fabric so the star pattern will also have a visual impact.

These instructions make a 12" (30.5 cm) finished block. Cutting instructions for a 6" (15 cm) finished block are included in the project section (page 139) Assembling the block is fast and easy when using the chainstitch technique, but be careful that you don't stretch the bias edges of the triangles.

How to Sew an Ohio Star Block

1 Cut four 5½" (14 cm) squares (page 54); two from star point fabric and two from background fabric. Cut five 4½" (11.5 cm) squares; four from background fabric and one from center fabric. Cut larger squares diagonally in both directions (page 63).

2 Place one background triangle on one star point triangle, right sides together. Stitch along one short side, using ¼" (6 mm) seam allowance; sew from right angle to point, and avoid stretching bias edges. Repeat seven times, chainstitching pairs (page 51).

3 Clip pairs apart. Align two pairs along their long side, right sides together; alternate fabrics and finger press seam allowances toward darker fabric. Pin at matched seams. Stitch; avoid stretching bias edges. Repeat three times, chainstitching units.

How to Sew an Ohio Star Block (cont.)

4 Clip the units apart. Press the seams. Trim off the points at each corner of the square.

5 Arrange four pieced squares and five plain squares as shown.

6 Chainstitch rows, right sides together; clip apart. Stitch rows together, finger pressing seam allowances in opposite directions; press those of middle row toward center square. Press block, turning long seams toward center square.

How to Sew a Churn Dash Block

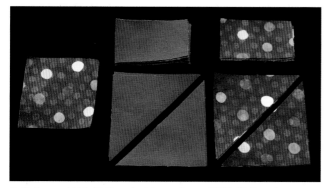

1 Cut one 1½" (3.8 cm) strip and two 2⅞" (7.2 cm) squares (page 54) from both the design and the background fabric; stack strips and squares. Cut four 1½" × 2½" (3.8 × 6.5 cm) rectangles from each strip. Cut squares diagonally in one direction. Cut one 2½" (6.5 cm) square from background fabric.

2 Align one design and one background triangle, right sides together. Stitch long side, using ¼" (6 mm) seam allowance; avoid stretching the bias edges. Repeat, chainstitching (page 51) remaining triangle pairs.

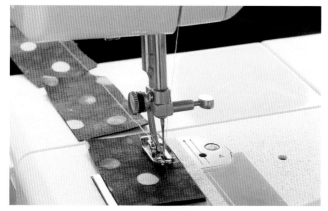

3 Align one design and one background rectangle, right sides together. Stitch one long side, using ¼" (6 mm) seam allowance. Chainstitch remaining rectangle pairs.

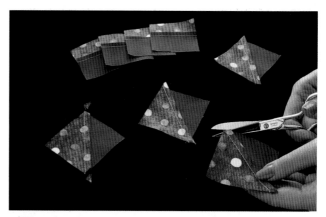

4 Clip triangle and rectangle pairs apart. Press seam allowances toward darker fabric. Trim points off corners of triangle-pieced squares.

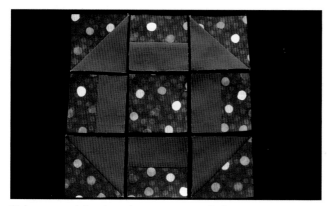

5 Arrange eight pieced squares around plain center square as shown.

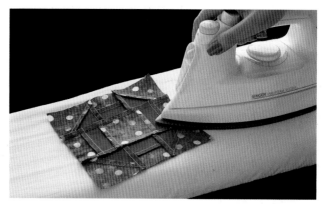

6 Chainstitch rows of squares, right sides together. Stitch rows together, finger pressing seam allowances in opposite directions; press those of middle row away from the center square. Press block, turning long seams away from center.

Appliqués

Appliqué quilts have traditionally required long and tedious hours of hand stitching. But quick machine-stitching methods save time without sacrificing the heirloom look.

Because appliqués frequently have curved and irregular shapes, they usually require templates for tracing the shapes onto the fabric. Templates for appliqués are made from cardboard and are cut to the exact size and shape of the finished appliqué. The templates do not include seam allowances; estimated ¼" (6 mm) seam allowances are added when the fabric is cut. The seam allowances are pressed around the template before stitching the appliqué, using spray starch to set the pressed seam allowances.

The appliqué is stitched to the background fabric, using the blindstitch on the sewing machine. Use the general-purpose or special-purpose foot and general-purpose needle plate. For invisible stitches, use fine, monofilament nylon thread in the needle and a thread that matches the background fabric in the bobbin. Loosen the needle thread tension so the bobbin thread does not show on the right side of the fabric and adjust the stitch width to about 1/16" (1.5 mm). Test the stitch setting on a sample appliqué.

It is important to keep the background fabric smooth during stitching. A piece of tear-away stabilizer placed under the background fabric during stitching helps to prevent the fabric from puckering. When pressing appliqués stitched with monofilament nylon thread, use a soleplate guard and a low-steam setting to prevent the thread from melting.

How to Sew Appliqués

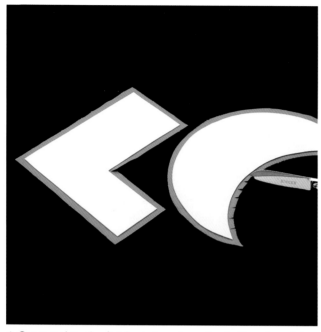

1 Cut template the finished size of appliqué. Place template on fabric. Cut around template using rotary cutter and adding ¼" (6 mm) seam allowance. Clip inside curves and corners almost to template.

2 Spray starch in small bowl; dab starch on section of seam allowance. With tip of iron, press seam allowance over edge of template; using dry iron, press until spray starch dries. Continue around appliqué. Remove template; press appliqué, right side up.

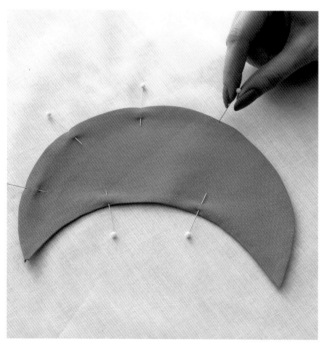

3 Pin or baste appliqué to background fabric.

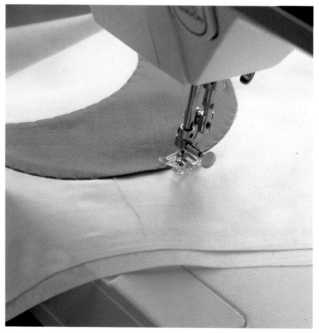

4 Set up machine (page 84). Blindstitch as close to appliqué as possible, just catching appliqué with widest swing of blindstitch. Turn stitch length to 0 and take three or four stitches to secure at ends. (Contrasting thread was used in photo to show detail.)

Harlequin Hearts Quilt Top

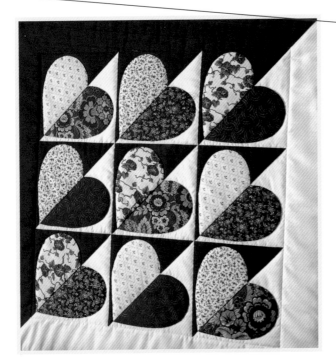

Make an attractive wall hanging, following the instructions for making the quilt blocks (pages 87 to 89). To complete the quilt top, stitch the border with mitered corners (page 96). To make a 27" (68.5 cm) square Harlequin Hearts quilt, you will need ¼ yard (0.25 m) each of six coordinating fabrics, three dark-colored and three light-colored, for the hearts. You will also need ½ yard (0.5 m) of the light-colored background and border fabric, ¾ yard (0.7 m) of the dark-colored background, border, and binding fabric, and ⅞ yard (0.8 m) of backing fabric.

Pattern for Harlequin Hearts Template

Template does not include seam allowances

Trace pattern actual size onto tracing paper and cut. Place on cardboard; trace and cut out template. Make sure, when tracing and cutting template, that edges are smooth and size is exact.

How to Make a Harlequin Hearts Quilt Top

1 Cut 8" (20.5 cm) strip (page 50) from each of two background fabrics; stack strips, matching edges. Cut five 8" (20.5 cm) squares from stack (page 51). Cut squares diagonally in half to make ten light and ten dark right triangles. For border, cut two 3½" × 28½" (9 × 72.3 cm) strips from each fabric.

2 Stack three layers of light-colored fabrics, right sides up. Place template on fabrics, straight edge on straight grain. Cut through all layers, adding a scant ¼" (6 mm) seam allowance along curved edge; do not add seam allowance on straight edge. Continue cutting to make nine half-hearts of light-colored fabric.

3 Stack three layers of dark-colored fabrics, right sides up. Turn template over; cut nine half-hearts, as in step 2. Turn under seam allowances on curved edges of all half-hearts, using spray starch method (page 85).

4 Pin one light half-heart to one dark triangle, right sides up, matching straight edges. Curved edges of heart will be ½" (1.3 cm) from sides of triangle. Repeat eight times to make nine units.

5 Place one dark half-heart on light half-heart unit, right sides together, matching edges of heart; pin at top and bottom along straight edge. Repeat eight times.

6 Place light triangle, right side down, over three-piece unit; pin. Stitch along center straight edges, through all layers, using ¼" (6 mm) seam allowance. Press seam allowances to dark side. Repeat eight times to make nine blocks.

7 Pin dark half-hearts to background fabric. Place tear-away stabilizer under block. Use monofilament thread in needle and match bobbin thread to the background fabric. Stitch, using blindstitching (page 85). Repeat for light half-hearts. (Contrasting thread was used in photo to show detail.)

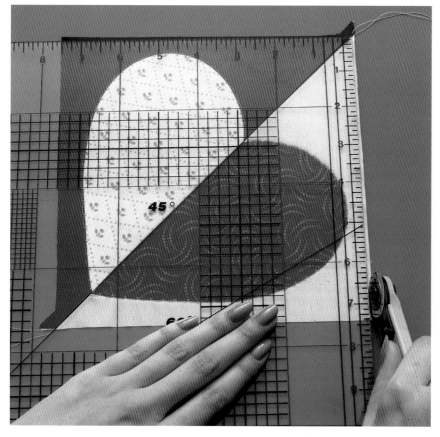

8 Remove tear-away stabilizer. Press blocks. Trim to exact 7½" (19.3 cm) squares. Stitch blocks, right sides together, in rows of three. Stitch rows together. Add border with mitered corners (page 96).

Sashing & Borders

Sashing separates the blocks in a quilt design, and borders frame the quilt. Both should be chosen carefully.

The sashing strips may be placed horizontally and vertically, or they may be placed diagonally. Once the blocks are completed, you may want to experiment with various widths of sashing. Sashing may be made from contrasting or background fabric and may be solid or pieced.

Make the final decision on a border design after the blocks and sashing are stitched together. A simple design that works well is a narrow, dark border next to the blocks, with a wide, lighter border around the outside. This sets off the piecing and unifies the quilt top.

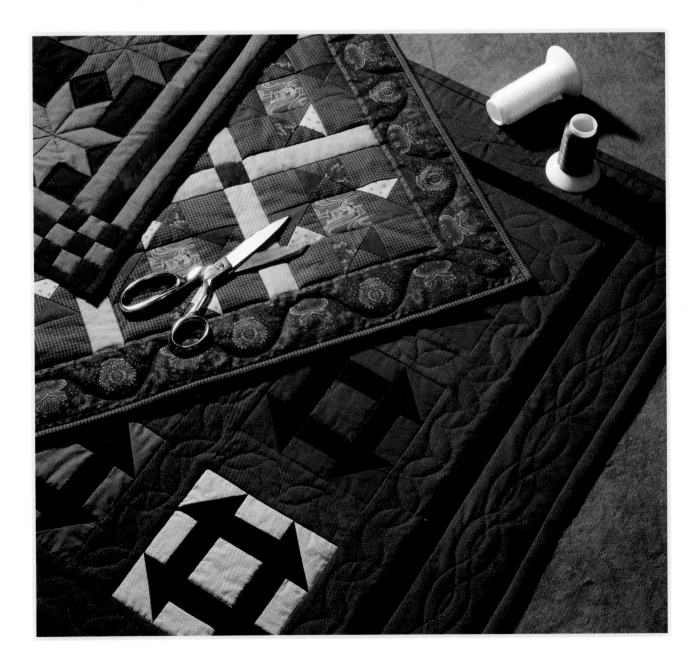

Sashing

Sashing strips frame individual quilt blocks and unify the entire quilt top. Sashing strips also change the finished size of a quilt. You can make a larger quilt from a small number of quilt blocks by adding sashing strips.

Plain sashing is a good choice for a quilt with a complex block design. Sashing with connecting squares adds more interest to a quilt. Use pieced connecting squares when the block design is less complex. The square can be any pieced design, such as a small nine-patch quilt block.

To determine the number of sashing strips required, refer to the sketch of the quilt top (page 32).

Specific measurements are not given in the instructions that follow, because the measurements are determined by the size of the blocks and the desired finished size of the quilt.

How to Make Plain Sashing Strips

1 Cut strips (page 50) to width specified in project directions. Or cut strips to desired width of sashing plus ½" (1.3 cm) for seam allowances.

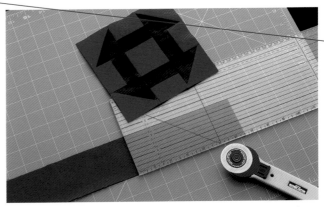

2 Measure all sides of several quilt blocks to determine the shortest measurement; cut short sashing strips to this length.

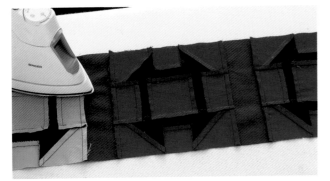

3 Stitch short sashing strips between blocks, right sides together, to form rows; do not stitch strips to ends of rows. Press seam allowances toward sashing.

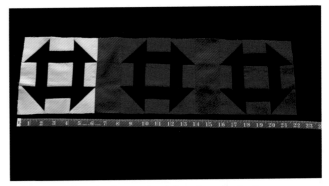

4 Measure length of rows to determine shortest measurement. Cut long sashing strips to this length, piecing as necessary.

5 Mark centers of sashing strips and rows. Place one long sashing strip along bottom of one row of blocks, right sides together; match and pin centers and ends. Pin along length, easing in any excess fullness; stitch. Repeat for remaining rows, except for bottom row.

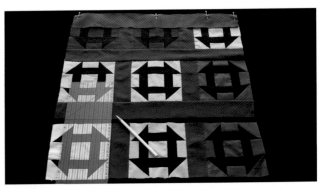

6 Align rows of blocks and mark sashing strips, as shown. Pin bottom of sashing strip to top of next row, right sides together; align marks to seamlines. Stitch as in step 5. Press seam allowances toward sashing. Continue until all rows are attached.

How to Make Sashing Strips with Connecting Squares

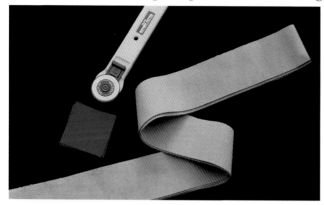

1 Cut strips (page 50) to width specified in project directions. Or cut strips to desired width of sashing plus ½" (1.3 cm) for seam allowances. Cut squares for corners from contrasting fabric the width of sashing strip.

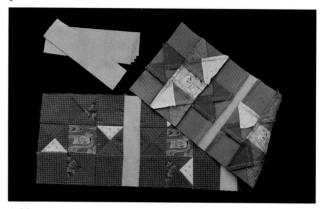

2 Measure all sides of several blocks to determine shortest measurement; cut sashing strips this length. Stitch strips between blocks, right sides together, to form rows; ease in fullness. Do not stitch strips to ends of rows. Press seam allowances toward strips.

3 Stitch the remaining sashing strips alternately to sashing squares, to equal length of block and sashing row. Press seam allowances toward sashing strips.

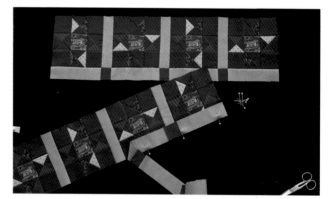

4 Place sashing unit along bottom of first row of blocks, right sides together, matching seams. Pin along length, easing in any fullness; stitch. Repeat for remaining rows, except for bottom row.

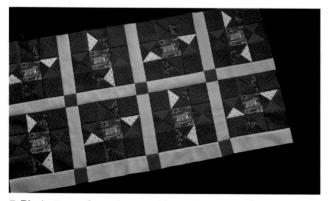

5 Pin bottom of one long sashing strip to top of next row, matching seams, as in step 4; stitch. Press seam allowances toward sashing strip. Continue until all rows are attached.

Alternate design. Make connecting checkerboard squares. Choose a width for sashing and finished squares that can be easily divided by 3. Use the nine-patch strip-piecing instructions (page 57).

Borders & Corners

Border strips can be cut on the crosswise or lengthwise grain of the fabric. Cutting them on the crosswise grain may save on the amount of fabric needed, but may require that the strips be pieced to make up the necessary length.

If the strips need to be pieced, the seams may be stitched either straight across the width of the strips, or diagonally on the bias; they may be placed in the center of the border. Seams can be concealed better in a printed fabric then in a solid-color fabric.

There are several ways to stitch corners of a border. The lapped corner is the simplest method. Mitered corners are frequently used for striped or border-print fabrics. Interrupted borders have a contrasting block at each corner, such as a nine-patch block.

Multiple borders are frequently used to incorporate more than one color from the quilt top. After the first border is stitched, the second border is added, using the same method. If lapped corners are used, they are lapped in the same direction on both borders.

How to Make a Lapped Corner

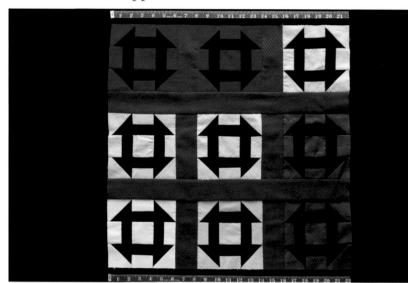

1 Measure top and bottom rows of quilt top. Cut two strips, with length of strips equal to shorter measurement, piecing as necessary; width of strips is equal to finished width of border plus ½" (1.3 cm).

2 Pin strip to upper edge of quilt top, right sides together, at center and at two ends; pin along length, easing in any fullness. Stitch; press seam allowance toward border. Repeat at lower edge.

3 Measure sides of the quilt top, including border strips. Cut two strips as in step 1. Pin and stitch to sides of quilt top as in step 2, including top and bottom border strips in seams.

How to Make a Border with Mitered Corners

1 Measure top and bottom rows of the quilt top to determine shorter measurement. Cut two strips, with length equal to shorter measurement plus 2 times finished width of border plus 1" (2.5 cm), and width equal to finished width of border plus ½" (1.3 cm)

2 Mark center of top and bottom rows and center of each border strip. From each end of border strip, mark the finished width of the border plus ½" (1.3 cm). Match center of one border strip to center of top edge of quilt top, right sides together; pin.

3 Match markings at ends of strip to edges of quilt top; pin. Continue pinning along edge, easing in any fullness. Stitch, beginning and ending ¼" (6 mm) from edges of quilt top; backstitch at ends. Repeat for bottom edge of quilt top.

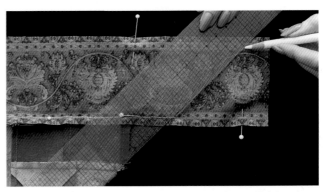

4 Repeat steps 1, 2 and 3 for sides or quilt top. Fold quilt top diagonally, right sides together, matching seamlines; pin securely. Draw diagonal line on border strip, extending line formed by fold or quilt top.

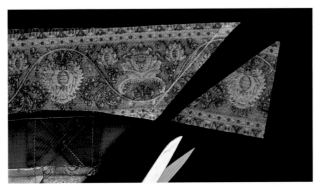

5 Stitch on marked line; do not catch seam allowances in stitching. Trim ends of border strips to ¼" (6 mm) seam allowances.

6 Press seam allowances open at corner; press remaining seam allowances toward border strip. Repeat for remaining corners.

How to Make a Border with Interrupted Corners

1 Measure top and bottom rows of the quilt top to determine the shorter measurement. Cut four strips of Fabric A and eight strips of Fabric B, with length equal to shorter measurement and width equal to one-third the finished width of border plus ½" (1.3 cm). Measure sides of quilt and cut strips.

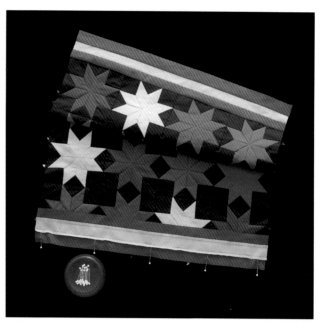

2 Sew strips together for top and bottom of quilt top to form two B-A-B units. Pin one pieced border to top of quilt, right sides together, at center and two ends; pin along length, easing in any fullness. Stitch. Press seam allowance toward border. Repeat with remaining unit at bottom.

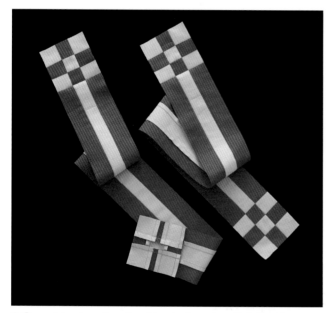

3 Sew strips together for sides to form two B-A-B units. Make four 9-patch blocks (page 57), using same width measurements as in step 1, above. Stitch one block to each end of border strips. Press seam allowances toward borders.

4 Pin and stitch the borders to sides of quilt, as in step 2, above, matching seams at corners. Press seam allowances toward border.

QUILTING

Types of Machine Quilting

Quilting holds the three layers of a quilt together, and adds design interest. Machine quilting is fast compared to hand quilting. You can quilt a project using the sewing machine in one-fourth to one-third the time it would take to do it by hand.

Machine quilting is strong, and the well-defined lines accentuate the quilting pattern. Machine stitches are tighter and compress the batting more than hand-quilting stitches, creating more depth and texture. Plan the quilting design to cover the surface uniformly. Whether you choose to quilt close together or far apart, keep your quilting evenly spaced across the entire top. Heavily quilted areas tend to shrink more than lightly quilted areas. There are three basic types of quilting: **tied (1)**, **machine-guided (2)**, **and freehand (3)**. Tying is a quick and easy way to finish a quilt. It is also the best way to maintain the loft of a thick batting. Traditionally, quilts were tied by hand with yarn or heavy thread, but a similar look can be achieved by using a sewing machine. In machine-guided quilting, the feed dogs and presser foot guide the fabric. This method is used for long, straight rows of stitches. In freehand quilting, the fabric is guided by hand; the feed dogs and presser foot are not used. In both machine-guided and freehand quilting, the stitching is an integral part of the quilt design and should be planned carefully. Quilting should reinforce or complement the piecing or appliqué design, and it should also form an appealing design on the back of the quilt.

Marking the Quilting Design

Quilting designs should be marked on the quilt top, unless the design follows the piecing or appliqué lines, as in echo or outline quilting.

Test the marking tools on the fabrics in the quilt top before marking. Be sure the marks can withstand handling, folding, and rolling, and that they can be thoroughly brushed, erased, or washed away after quilting.

It is easier to mark the quilt top before the layers are basted together. Place the quilt top on a hard, flat surface and draw or trace the design accurately with a clear, thin line.

If you are using a template to mark the design on a border, mark the corners first. If a design of repeating motifs does not fit, adjust the length of several motifs as necessary. You can use a single motif at the corners of the border or mark intersecting lines of channel quilting (page 115) to form a grid.

Guides used for making quilting lines are rulers and plastic templates.

How to Mark a Quilting Design

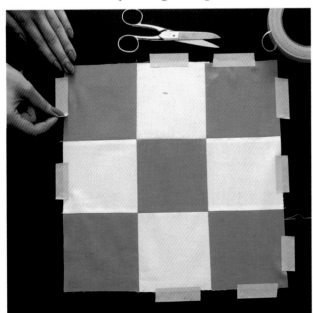

1 Press quilt top; place on hard, flat work surface, with corners square and sides parallel. Tape securely, keeping quilt top smooth and taut.

2 Mark quilting design, using ruler or template as a guide, beginning in corners. Mark distinct, thin lines, using as light a touch as possible.

Batting & Backing

Although batting is available in different sizes, it may need to be pieced for larger projects. Battings differ in loft and fiber content (pages 40 and 41). Loft is the thickness and springiness of a batting. It determines the degree of texture in a quilt.

The batting and backing should extend 2" to 4" (5 to 10 cm) beyond the edges of the quilt top on all sides, to allow for the shrinkage that occurs during quilting. It may be necessary to piece the batting and backing.

How to Piece Batting and Backing Fabric

1 **Batting.** Overlap two pieces of batting, 1" to 2" (2.5 to 5 cm).

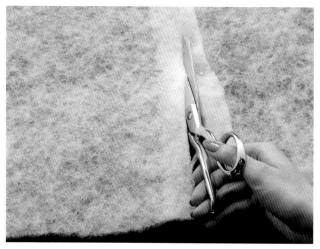

2 **Cut** with shears through both layers, down the center of overlapped section.

3 **Remove** trimmed edges. Butt batting edges, and whipstitch by hand to secure.

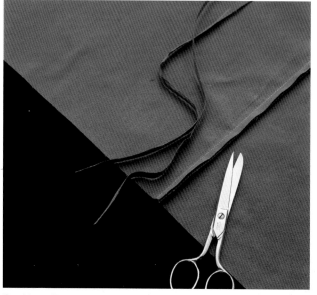

Backing Cut selvages from fabric. Piece fabric as necessary, positioning seams as on page 35. Stitch, using a stitch length of 12 to 15 stitches per inch (2.5 cm) and ¼" (6 mm) seam allowances. Press seam allowances to one side or open.

Basting the Layers for Quilting

Basting keeps the three layers of the quilt from shifting during the quilting process. Traditionally, quilts were basted using needle and thread; however, safety-pin basting may be used instead.

Lay the quilt out flat on a hard surface, such as the floor or a large table and baste the entire quilt. Or baste the quilt in sections on a table at least one-fourth the size of the quilt.

Press the quilt top and backing fabric flat before layering and basting. If basting with safety pins, use 1" (2.5 cm) rustproof steel pins. Steel pins glide through fabrics more easily than brass pins, and the 1" (2.5 cm) size is easier to handle.

If basting with thread, use white cotton thread and a large milliners' or darning needle. Use a large running stitch, about 1" (2.5 cm) long. Pull the stitches snug so the layers will not shift. Backstitch at the ends to secure the stitching.

How to Baste a Quilt on a Surface Larger Than the Quilt

1 Fold quilt top, right sides together, into quarters, without creasing. Mark center of each side at raw edges with safety pins. Repeat for batting and backing, folding backing wrong sides together.

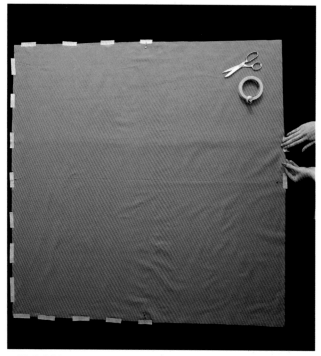

2 Unfold backing on work surface, wrong side up. Tape securely, beginning at center of each side and working toward corners, stretching fabric slightly. Backing should be taut, but not overly stretched.

3 Place batting on backing, matching pins on each side. Smooth, but do not stretch, working from center of quilt out to sides.

4 Place quilt top, right side up, on batting, matching pins on each side; smooth, but do not stretch.

5 Baste with pins or thread from center of quilt to pins on sides; if thread-basting, pull stitches snug so layers will not shift. Avoid basting on marked quilting lines or through seams.

6 Baste one quarter section in parallel rows about 6" (15 cm) apart, working toward raw edges. If thread-basting, also baste quarter-section in parallel rows in opposite direction, as shown in step 2, opposite.

7 Repeat step 6 for remaining quarter sections. Remove tape from backing.

8 Fold edges of backing over batting and edges of quilt top to prevent raw edges of fabric from raveling and batting from catching on needle and feed dogs during quilting. Pin-baste.

How to Baste a Quilt on a Surface Smaller Than the Quilt

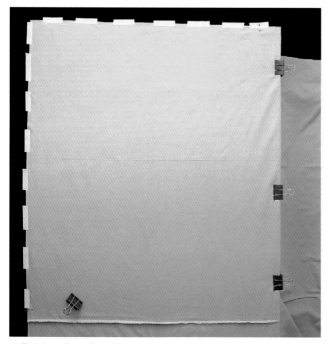

1 Fold and mark quilt as in step 1, page 103. Lay backing on table, wrong side up; let sides hang over edge of table. Tape raw edges of backing to tabletop. Clamp backing securely to table, stretching slightly, beginning at center of each side and working toward corners; place clamps about 12" (30.5 cm) apart.

2 Place batting on backing, matching pins on each side. Place quilt top right side up on batting, matching pins on each side; smooth, but do not stretch. Baste one quarter section of quilt as in steps 5 and 6, opposite. Remove tape and clamps.

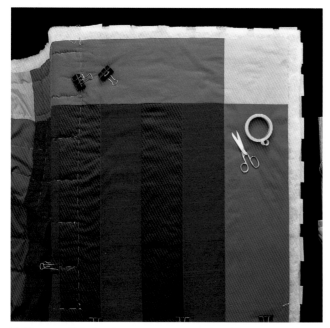

3 Move quilt to baste next quarter section. Tape raw edges of backing to tabletop, stretching slightly; clamp all layers of quilt to edges of table. Baste quarter section as in steps 5 and 6, opposite.

4 Repeat for remaining quarter sections. Check for any tucks on backing; rebaste as necessary. Fold and pin-baste edges as in step 8, opposite.

Machine Quilting Basics

When machine-quilting, it is necessary to roll or fold the quilt in order for it to fit under the sewing machine head and to prevent it from hanging over the edge of the table. You may want to expand your sewing surface to support the quilt (page 47).

Always keep the largest section of quilt to the left of the needle as you stitch. As you quilt from the center toward the sides, there is less fabric to feed under the head of the machine, making the quilt easier to manage.

Cotton or monofilament nylon thread may be used for quilting (page 44). If using monofilament nylon thread, use it only in the needle and use a thread that matches the backing fabric in the bobbin. Loosen the needle thread tension so the bobbin thread does not show on the right side.

When machine quilting, stitch continuously, minimizing starts and stops as much as possible. Check for any tucks in the backing by feeling through the layers of the quilt ahead of the sewing machine needle. Prevent the tucks from being stitched by continuously easing in the excess fabric before it reaches the needle. If a tuck does occur, release stitches for 3" (7.5 cm) or more, and restitch, easing in excess fabric.

Quilting Sequence

Plan the stitching sequence before you begin to quilt. First quilt the longest or largest sections, working from the center toward the sides. For example, for a quilt with sashing, quilt the sashing strips before quilting the blocks, starting with the center strips and working toward the side strips. This helps anchor the layers throughout the quilt to prevent them from shifting.

Next, quilt the areas within the blocks that will not be heavily quilted, such as motifs. Then proceed to the smaller areas or those that will be more heavily quilted.

The sequence for quilting varies with the style of the quilt. For quilts with side-by-side blocks, anchor the layers throughout the quilt by stitching in the ditch between the blocks in vertical and horizontal rows. For a medallion quilt, stitch in the ditch along the border seam to anchor the layers; then quilt the central area.

How to Prepare a Large Quilt for Machine Quilting

1 Lay the quilt flat, right side up. For quilts with polyester batting, roll one side to within 2" or 3" (5 or 7.5 cm) of center basting line. If necessary, secure roll with larger safety pins or plastic headband. For quilts with cotton batting, loosely fold one side into accordion folds; it will stay without pins.

2 Roll or fold other side, as in step 1, if the sewing surface is not large enough to hold remaining width of quilt flat.

How to Prepare a Large Quilt for Machine Quilting (cont.)

3 Fold quilt loosely along length, accordion-style, into lap-size bundle. Place bundle on your lap.

4 Pull quilt up from lap, section by section, so it is level with needle as you stitch. Do not allow quilt to hang over back or side of sewing table.

Tips for Quilting

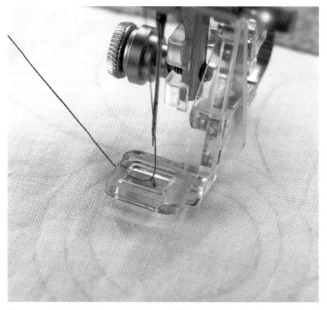

Draw up bobbin thread to the quilt top by turning handwheel by hand, and stopping with needle at highest position. Pull on needle thread to bring the bobbin thread up through fabric.

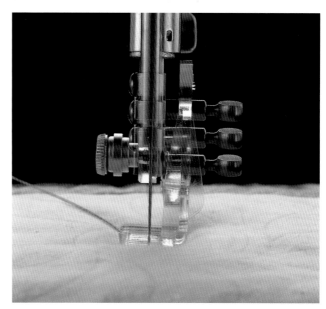

Stitch in place several times to secure stitches at beginning and end of stitching lines for freehand quilting. For machine-guided quilting, begin stitching with stitch length set at 0. Gradually increase stitch length for about ½" (1.3 cm) to desired stitch length. Reverse procedure at end of stitching line.

Freehand quilting. Position hands so they act as a hoop, encircling needle. Gently press down and pull outward to create tension on fabric. Move fabric with wrist and hand movements as you stitch. Rest elbows comfortably on sewing table while stitching; it may be helpful to elevate elbows on books.

Machine-guided quilting. Position hands on either side of presser foot. Gently press down and hold fabric taut to prevent layers from shifting, causing puckers or tucks. Ease any excess fabric under the presser foot as you stitch.

Machine-Tying a Quilt

When using a high-loft batting, machine-tie the quilt to preserve the loft. A quilt can be machine-tied by using a zigzag or decorative stitch, or by attaching ribbons or yarns.

Mark the placement of the ties on the quilt top before basting it to the batting and backing. Stagger the rows of ties for greater interest and strength. Space the ties approximately 5" (12.5 cm) apart.

Three Ways to Tie a Quilt by Machine

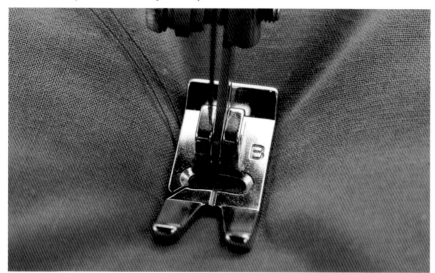

Zigzag stitch. Adjust stitch length and width to 0. Holding threads behind needle, stitch several times through all layers. Adjust stitch width to a wide setting; stitch 8 to 10 times. Return Stitch width to 0; stitch several times. Clip threads.

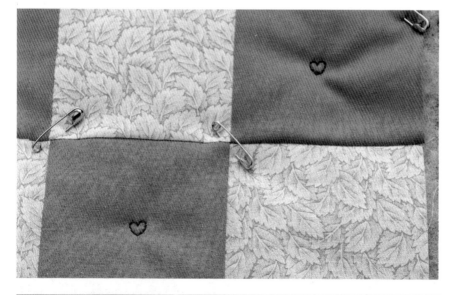

Decorative stitch. Use a decorative stitch instead of a zigzag stitch to secure quilt layers; adjust stitch length and width for an attractive design. Stitch in place at beginning and end of decorative stitch.

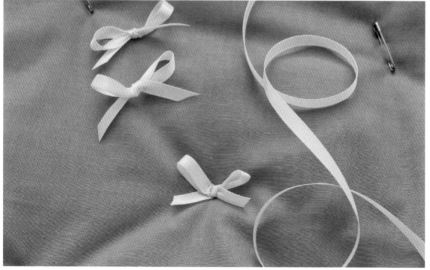

Ribbon or yarn. Cut one 3" to 6" (7.5 to 15 cm) length of ribbon for each tie. Tie into bow. Center bow over placement mark; stitch bow in place, using zigzag stitch, above.

Machine-Guided Quilting

Machine-guided quilting uses pressure from the feed dogs and presser foot to guide the three layers of fabric through the sewing machine. The Even Feed foot helps to prevent tucks when quilting.

Machine-guided quilting is used for stitching long lines of quilting. A straight stitch is most commonly used, but any stitch will work, including decorative stitches. Practice on the sample to determine the appropriate stitch length and width. Space the stitching lines according to the type of batting used (page 41).

Grid quilting (1) is stitched in evenly spaced lines. The quilting lines can be diagonal in both directions, or both vertical and horizontal. Diagonal quilting lines are marked, as shown opposite. You may want to draw the grid lines on paper before marking the actual quilt top to become familiar with the technique. The paper can be cut to the size of the quilt or in proportion to it.

Stitch-in-the-ditch quilting (2) emphasizes the pieced design, because it is stitched following the seamlines for the blocks, across length and width of quilt.

Outline quilting (3) also emphasizes the pieced design. It is stitched ¼" (6 mm) from the seamlines, outlining the pieces or blocks. Outline quilting can be either machine-guided or freehand. Use machine-guided quilting when the project is small enough so the quilt can be turned easily. For lines of stitching that change direction a lot, such as small squares or triangles, freehand outline quilting (pages 116 to 119) is easier.

Channel quilting (4) is stitched in evenly spaced lines. The quilting lines can be either diagonal, vertical, or horizontal. The quilting lines are marked using a ruler, as on page 113.

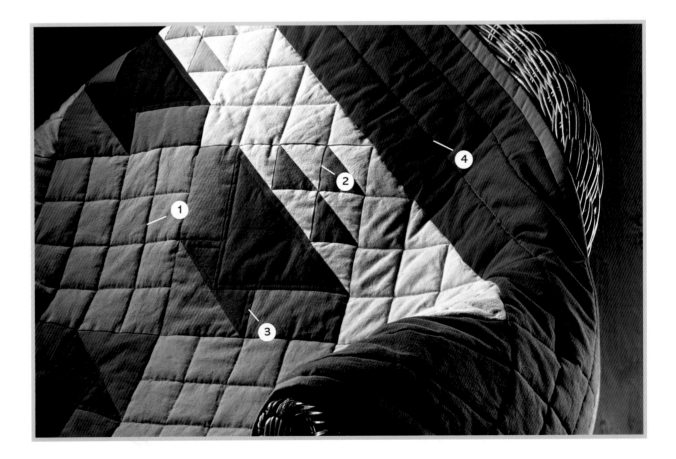

How to Grid-quilt on the Diagonal

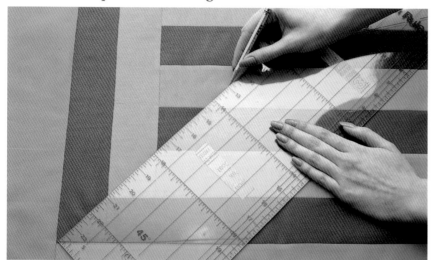

1 Tape quilt top to flat surface and mark quilting lines before basting quilt. Mark first line at an exact 45-degree angle to edge of design, starting at one corner; continue line to edge of design on opposite side.

2 Mark a line from end of previous line to opposite edge, keeping marked lines at 90-degree angles to each other and 45-degree angle to edge of design; continue marking lines in this manner until a line ends at a corner.

3 Mark a line, starting from another corner, if lines do not yet complete the grid design; continue marking lines to form a grid.

How to Grid-quilt on the Diagonal (cont.)

4 Mark additional quilting lines halfway between grid marks and parallel to previous lines, if smaller grid is desired.

5 Place quilt layers together and baste (pages 102 to 105). Stitch on marked lines, starting in one corner.

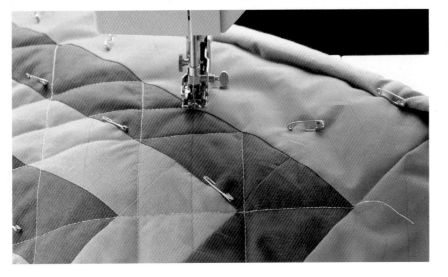

6 Stitch lines in same sequence as marked; turn fabric 90 degrees at edge of design, pivoting with needle down.

How to Outline-quilt

Stitch about ¼" (6 mm) from seamline, starting at corner. To prevent puckers and tucks, feed fabric under presser foot (page 109).

How to Stitch-in-the-ditch-quilt

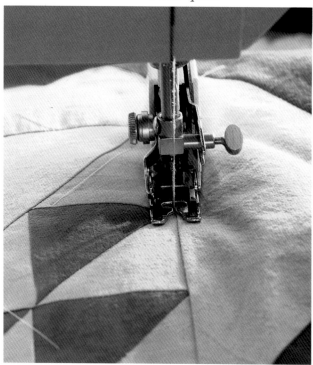

Stitch in the ditch so stitches are hidden in the seam. To prevent puckers and tucks, feed fabric under presser foot (page 109).

How to Channel-quilt

1 Stitch lengthwise, on marked quilting line, at center of area to be quilted. Stitch parallel lines, working from center toward right side.

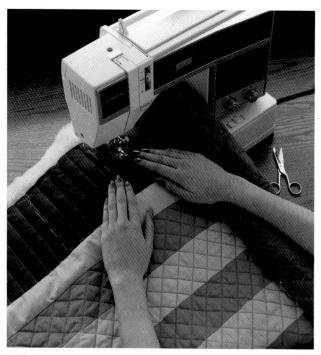

2 Turn quilt 180 degrees. Stitch parallel lines, working from center toward right side, to complete quilting.

Freehand Quilting

Freehand quilting is done by guiding the quilt through the machine by hand. Since you control the movement of the fabric, you can stitch in any direction without repositioning the quilt. This makes freehand quilting appropriate for designs with sharp turns and intricate curves, such as outline, motif, and background quilting. You may want to practice freehand quilting before stitching on the actual quilt.

For freehand quilting, set the machine for straight stitching and use a straight-stitch needle plate; cover the feed dogs or lower them. You may use a darning foot, if desired, or stitch without a presser foot. Lower the presser foot lifter even if a presser foot is not used.

The stitch length is determined by a combination of the movement of the quilt and the speed of the needle. Maintain a steady rhythm and speed as you stitch, to keep the stitch length uniform. In freehand quilting, the objective is to stitch as far as you can without stopping. Look at the overall design to determine the continuous stitching lines (pages 118). You may want to sketch the quilt design on paper and, using a pencil, plan some stitching sequences.

Outline quilting (1) follows the patterns established by piecing and emphasizes the lines of the pieced design.

Motif quilting (2) uses shapes and design elements, such as hearts and wreaths. It is usually done in open areas of a quilt top, such as borders and plain blocks. Quilting stencils are available for many designs. For continuous stitching of motifs, it may be necessary to double-stitch small areas, but the loft of the batting usually conceals double-stitched lines that are less than 2" (5 cm) long.

Echo quilting (3) and **stipple quilting** (4) are types of background quilting. They require a minimum of starting and stopping and can be done without marking the quilt top. Background quilting adds a uniform texture to a section of the quilt. Echo quilting repeats the lines of a motif or appliqué, each row of stitching around it getting larger. Stipple quilting is random stitching that fills in the background. You can get a very compact look by keeping stitching lines close together. Keep the density of the stitching consistent throughout the area.

Combination quilting (5) uses outline or motif quilting as the dominant element in the blocks, with background quilting filling the remainder of the surface. By combining different types of quilting, you can highlight or emphasize specific areas of the quilt design.

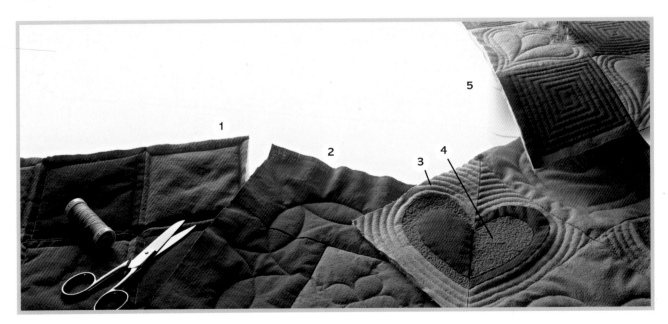

How to Outline-quilt

1 Sketch block and draw quilting lines ¼" (6 mm) from seamlines. Connect corners of quilting lines to intersecting seamlines.

2 Determine the longest continuous stitching line; mark starting point and directional stitching arrows on sketch.

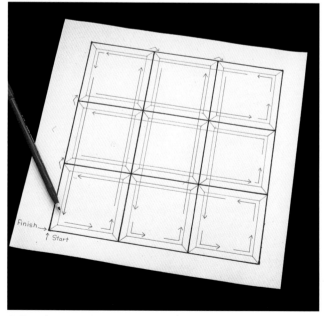

3 Continue marking directional stitching arrows on sketch and mark end point.

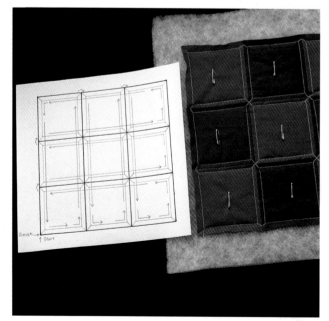

4 Mark quilting lines on quilt top. Place quilt layers together and baste (pages 102 to 105). Stitch on marked lines, double-stitching diagonally in and out of corners as necessary.

How to Quilt a Single Motif

1 Draw quilting design on paper. Determine the longest continuous stitching line; mark starting point, directional stitching arrows, and end point on sketch.

2 Mark motif on quilt top. Place quilt layers together and baste (pages 102 to 105). Stitch on marked lines; secure stitches at beginning and end of stitching lines by stitching in place.

How to Quilt a Row of Connecting Motifs

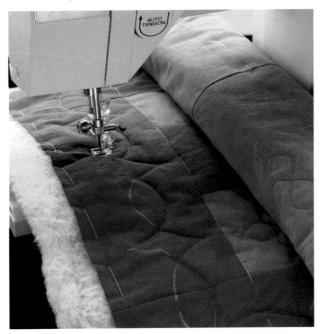

Mark motifs on quilt top. Place quilt layers together and baste (pages 102 to 105). Stitch motifs above points where motifs connect. Return to starting point; stitch motifs below connecting points.

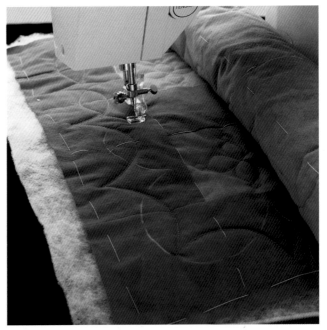

Alternate method. Stitch top of first motif, then bottom of second motif, and back to top of third motif. Continue in this manner to end. Return to starting point and complete motifs.

How to Echo-quilt

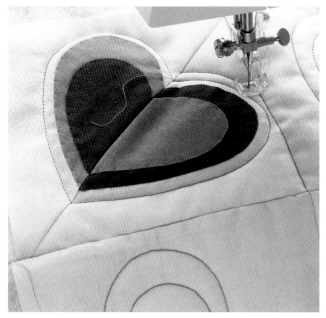

Stitch around motif, approximately ¼" (6 mm) from edges. Secure threads by stitching in place. Raise needle to highest position, lift the presser foot, and move fabric over ¼" (6 mm). Repeat until quilting design is completed.

Alternate method. Stitch in a spiral design, spacing lines approximately ¼" (6 mm) apart.

How to Stipple-quilt

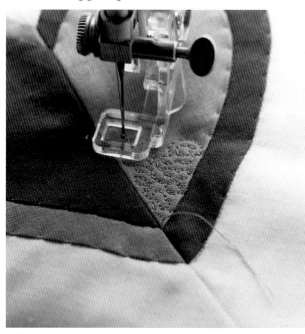

1 Work in small sections, about the size of a quarter. Stitch curvy, meandering lines.

2 Work from the edges toward the center, covering background uniformly.

Binding a Quilt

There are several methods for finishing the edges of a quilt. For mock binding, fold the backing fabric over the raw edges to the quilt top. For double binding with lapped corners, attach a separate strip of binding fabric to each edge and overlap the binding at the corners. Double binding can also be applied in one continuous strip, forming miters at each corner.

Mock binding is an easy way to finish the edges of a quilt and makes use of the excess backing fabric needed during basting and quilting. Choose a backing fabric that coordinates with the quilt top. Double binding is cut on the straight of grain and has two layers of fabric to provide a durable edge. The binding can either match or complement the quilt top. For all three methods, the finished binding is ½" (1.3 cm) wide.

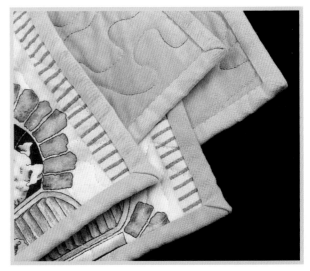

Double binding with mitered corners.

Mock binding (top) and double binding with lapped corners (bottom).

How to Bind a Quilt with Mock Binding

1 Machine-baste through all layers of the quilt, ⅛" (3 mm) from raw edges of quilt top.

2 Trim batting only, ¼" (6 mm) from edge of quilt top, ⅜" (1 cm) from basting stitches.

3 Trim backing 1" (2.5 cm) from cut edge of batting.

4 Fold backing diagonally at corner of batting; press foldline.

How to Bind a Quilt with Mock Binding (cont.)

5 Fold backing so edge of backing meets edge of batting; press.

6 Fold backing over edge of batting and quilt top, covering stitching line; pin.

7 Cut out square of excess fabric at each corner. Pin corners.

8 Edgestitch along fold to secure. Remove basting stitches on quilt back. Slipstitch corners, if desired.

How to Bind a Quilt with Double Lapped Binding

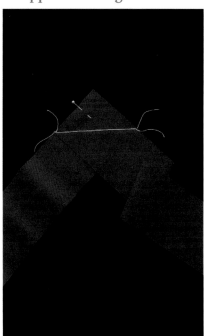

1 Fold fabric in half on lengthwise grainline (page 50). Cut strips 3" (7.5 cm) on crosswise grainline.

2 Pin strips, right sides together, at right angles; strips will form a V. Stitch diagonally across strips.

3. Trim the seam allowances to ¼" (6 mm). Press seam open. Trim points even with edges.

4 Measure one side of quilt; cut binding this length plus 2" (5 cm). Mark binding 1" (2.5 cm) in from each end; divide section between pins in quarters; pin-mark. Divide sides of quilt in quarters; pin-mark.

5 Fold binding in half lengthwise, wrong sides together. Place binding on quilt top, matching raw edges and pin-marks; binding will extend 1" (2.5 cm) beyond quilt top at each end.

6 Stitch binding to quilt ¼" (6 mm) from raw edges of binding.

How to Bind a Quilt with Double Lapped Binding (cont.)

7 Cut excess batting and backing to ½" (1.3 cm) from stitching line.

8 Wrap binding around edge of quilt, covering stitching line on back of quilt; pin.

9 Stitch in the ditch on the right side of quilt, catching binding on back of quilt.

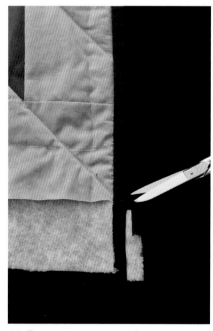

10 Repeat steps 4 to 9 for opposite side of quilt. Trim ends of binding even with edges of quilt top.

11 Repeat steps 4 to 7 for remaining two sides. Trim ends of binding to extend ½" (1.3 cm) beyond finished edges of quilt.

12 Fold binding down along the stitching line. Fold ½" (1.3 cm) end of binding over finished edge; press in place. Wrap binding around edge and stitch in the ditch as in steps 8 and 9. Slipstitch end by hand.

How to Bind a Quilt with Double Mitered Binding

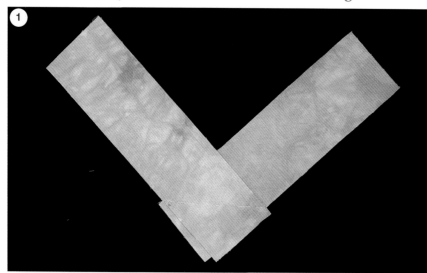

1 Trim the batting and backing even with the edges of the quilt top. Measure perimeter of quilt; add 12" (30.5 cm). Divide the measurement by 40" (101.5 cm) to calculate the number of strips needed. Cut 2¼" (5.7 cm) wide strips from selvage to selvage (crosswise grain). Pin strips, right sides together, at right angles; strips will form a V. Stitch diagonally across strips.

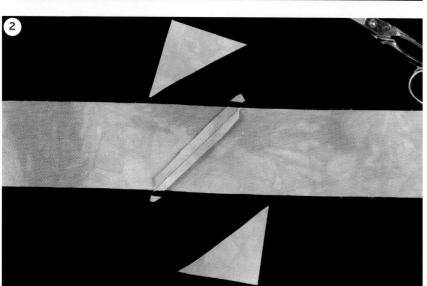

2 Trim seam allowances to ¼" (6 mm). Press seam open. Trim points even edges.

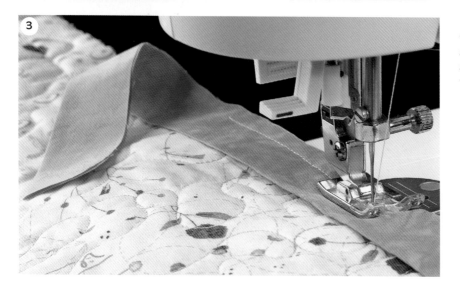

3 Fold binding in half lengthwise, wrong sides together; press. Lay binding along the edge of the quilt top. Leave an 8" tail, stitch the binding in place with about ¼" (6 mm) seam allowance.

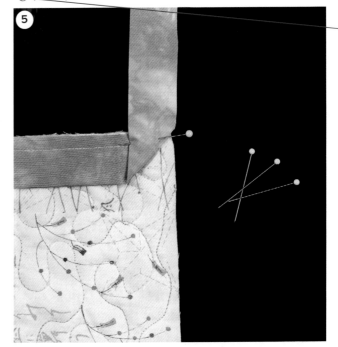

4 Stop sewing ¼" (6 mm) from the corner of the quilt. With needle in down position, pivot quilt top and stitch diagonally to the corner of the quilt. Clip the thread.

5 Fold the binding up and away from the quilt top.

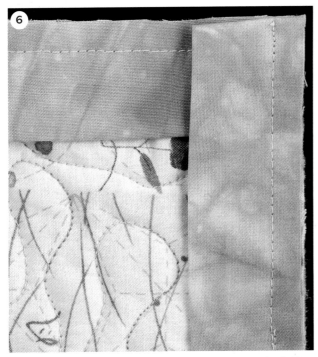

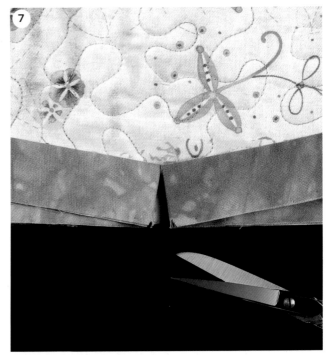

6 Fold the binding back down onto itself; keeping the fold aligned with the edge of the quilt top. Begin stitching from the upper fold, and continue to the next corner. Repeat steps 4 to 6 for the remaining edges.

7 Stop sewing 8" (20.3 cm) from the starting point; remove the quilt from the sewing machine and lay quilt on flat surface. Fold the two tail ends back on themselves so they meet in the middle of the unsewn edge. Clip ⅛" (3 mm) notches into bindings at the meeting point.

8 On the end tail, measure 2¼"
(5.7 cm) from notch and cut a second
set of notches.

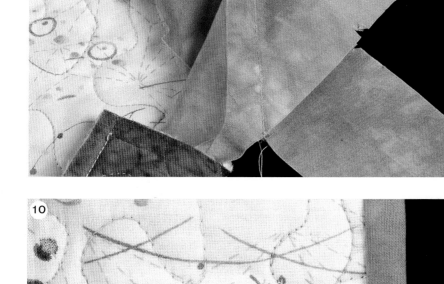

9 Position the quilt to the left, and
binding and quilt edge on the right.
With your left hand, open the end tail
so the right side is facing you. With
your right hand, open the start tail with
wrong side facing you. Lay the start
tail on top of the end tail at a diagonal;
right sides together; notches matching
on raw edges of binding. Pin in place;
mark diagonal line. Sew on marked
edge. Finger press the seam open;
check for accuracy before trimming
seam to ¼" (6 mm).

10. Finish stitching the binding to the
quilt top. Fold the binding over the raw
edges to the back. Blindstich binding
in place, with the folded edge covering
the line of machine stitching. A miter
will form at each corner. Blindstich the
mitered corner in place.

Quilt Care

Whether you value your quilt as a family heirloom or a work of art, you will want to take care of it so that it retains its beauty for a long time. Even quilts that are handled and used daily will last longer if you clean and store them with care.

Displaying Quilts

A popular way to display a quilt is to hang it on a wall. Any method for hanging a quilt places some stress on it, but attaching a fabric sleeve to the back distributes the weight evenly.

When choosing a place to display a quilt, avoid direct sunlight or bright, constant artificial light. If you display the quilt on a wooden shelf or quilt rack, place a double piece of washed, unbleached muslin between the wood and the quilt, or seal the wood with paint or polyurethane varnish.

If the quilt will be used to cover a table, you may want to protect the top of the quilt with glass or plexiglass cut to shape; air the quilt regularly to prevent mold and mildew. Also, shift the position of the quilt occasionally to keep permanent creases from forming.

If the quilts are folded and stacked for display in an open cupboard, pad the folds with washed, unbleached muslin or acid-free tissue paper. Refold the quilts periodically so fabric does not fade at the fold lines.

How to Hang a Quilt Using a Fabric Sleeve

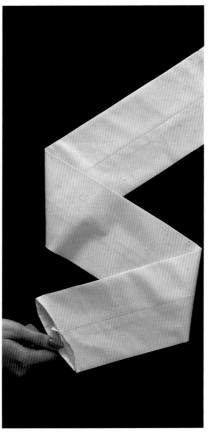

1 Cut piece of washed, unbleached muslin, 10" (25.5 cm) wide by the width of the quilt. Turn under and stitch double ½" (1.3 cm) hems at short ends.

2 Stitch long edges of strip, right sides together, using ½" (1.3 cm) seam; press seam allowances open. Turn sleeve right side out; press flat, centering seam along back.

3 Pin sleeve to back of quilt, close to edges. Blindstitch sleeve to quilt along top and bottom edges; stitch through backing and batting. Insert sealed wooden lattice through sleeve, not between quilt and sleeve.

Cleaning Quilts

The care of a quilt depends on how it is used. If you are making a quilt to hang on the wall, it may only need to be vacuumed or shaken out occasionally. If you are making a quilt to be used on the bed, it will be laundered periodically. The less a quilt is handled, the longer it will last. Fabrics are easily damaged by abrasion and stress.

Dust and dirt abrade the fibers and shorten the life of a quilt. Quilts may be cleaned by vacuuming them, or by laundering them by machine or by hand. Dry cleaning is not recommended for washable fabrics, especially cottons; the chemicals used in dry cleaning may react with some dyes, resulting in color changes.

Vacuuming keeps quilts clean and minimizes the need to wash them. It is recommended that you lay the quilt on a flat, padded surface and vacuum it gently, using an upholstery brush and low suction. To protect the quilt from abrasion, you may place a fiberglass screen over the quilt and vacuum it through the screen.

Wash and dry quilts only when absolutely necessary, because washing and drying place stress on the fabric, particularly when done by machine. Before washing a quilt, test all dark and vivid fabrics for colorfastness (page 39).

Hand washing is gentler on the fabric, but quilts made of washable fabrics and battings may be washed and dried by machine. Whether you wash a quilt by hand or by machine, use mild soap without perfumes and other additives, such as dishwashing soap. Avoid soaps and detergents recommended for washing fine woolens; they may yellow cotton fabrics.

Tips for Washing and Drying Quilts

Machine Washing and Drying

Use large washing machine and high water level.

Wash on gentle or delicate cycle.

Remove quilt from washing machine immediately after washing, or wet fabrics may bleed.

Dry on cool to warm setting. Place dry terrycloth towel in dryer with quilt to shorten drying time.

Remove quilt from dryer before it is completely dry; spread flat on clean cloth, smoothing out wrinkles, to finish drying. Do not press.

Hand Washing and Drying

Use large tub, to keep quilt as flat as possible; for large quilts, use bathtub.

Place quilt flat in tub, or in loose folds, as necessary.

Wash gently by hand, using a kneading motion; do not bunch, swirl, or twist.

Drain water, and refill tub with clear water; do not lift quilt. Repeat process until soap is rinsed out completely.

Press out remaining water, gently squeezing quilt against tub, working toward the drain. Blot with clean towels or mattress pad to remove excess water.

Lay quilt flat on clean sheets or mattress pad to dry. If drying quilt outdoors, avoid direct sunlight and cover quilt with clean sheet to protect it. If drying quilt indoors, use a fan to shorten drying time.

Thoroughly dissolve the soap and fill the machine or tub with lukewarm water before adding the quilt. Be sure there is enough water to cover the quilt, to help disperse any excess dye and aid in cleaning and rinsing. It is important to rinse all the soap out of the fabric; soap residue can coat the fibers, attracting dirt and discoloring the fabric.

Use extra care in handling a quilt while it is wet. Water adds weight, so, rather than pick up a wet quilt by a corner or edge, support the entire quilt in your arms or in a towel. Lay the quilt flat to air-dry instead of hanging it. Quilts may also be dried by machine. Machine drying fluffs the batting, but air drying is less abrasive to the fabric.

Storing Quilts

The best way to store a quilt is to keep it flat on a bed. Quilts usually suffer less damage from use than from storage. The most common forms of damage are fading, fabric deterioration, staining, and permanent creasing.

Fading of fabrics is caused primarily by exposure to light. Light also damages fabric over a period of time, making it brittle and weak.

Mold and mildew can cause staining, so quilts should be stored at a humidity of 45 to 50 percent. Staining and deterioration can also occur when quilts come in contact with storage materials such as paper and wood. As these materials age, they release chemicals that destroy fabrics. Acid-free papers and boxes are available for storing quilts. Permanent creases are caused by folding and by pressure. When a quilt is folded for storage, the fibers along the folded edge are weakened and may break; the sharper the fold, the greater the damage. Putting weight on top of folded quilts increases the damage. Therefore, if you stack quilts in storage, refold and rotate the order occasionally.

Pad folds of quilt with acid-free tissue paper or with washed, unbleached cotton fabric to prevent sharp creases. Refold quilts every few months, changing the placement of fold lines.

Tips for Storing Quilts

Clean quilts thoroughly before storing.

Store quilts in washed, unbleached muslin or cotton pillowcases or sheets. Acid-free tubes, tissue paper, or boxes may also be used; these may be obtained from archival storage mail-order sources or from some quilt stores.

Seal wood that will come in contact with quilts, using paint or polyurethane varnish.

Avoid exposing quilts to direct sunlight to keep fabrics from fading and becoming brittle.

Avoid storing quilts in places where the humidity is high or where the temperature fluctuates greatly, such as attics or basements. Dry quilts thoroughly if they have become damp.

Do not store quilts in plastic bags.

Keep quilts away from direct heat sources, such as radiators, heat registers, or sunlight.

Project Directions

A materials list and complete directions for creating each project shown in the book are provided below and on the following pages.

General Directions

1. **Cut** and stitch blocks, pieced strips, or individual units, following specific project directions.
2. **Arrange** quilt top as shown. Stitch any sashing strips between blocks or pieced strips, and rows (pages 92 to 93).
3. **Stitch** borders to quilt top (pages 94 to 97).

4. **Mark** quilting design on blocks, sashing, and border strips (page 100) as desired; you may choose to quilt areas that have not been quilted in the samples. Stitch-in-the-ditch quilting does not require marking.
5. **Baste** quilt layers together (pages 102 to 105).
6. **Machine-quilt** layers together (pages 113 to 119).
7. **Bind** quilt (pages 120 to 127).

How to Make a Sampler Quilt

(Shown on page 13.) Finished size: 50" (127 cm) square; nine 12" (30.5 cm) blocks are used.

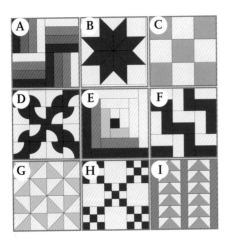

YOU WILL NEED

1 yd. (0.95 m) light background fabric A, for blocks.

1½ yd. (1.4 m) print fabric B, for blocks and borders.

¼ yd. (0.25 m) each of four different prints, for blocks; label prints C, D, E, and F.

1¼ yd. (1.15 m) fabric G, for log cabin center, sashing, and binding.

Backing fabric, 54" (137 cm) square.

Batting, 54" (137 cm) square.

Cutting Directions

Cut four 3½" (9 cm) lengthwise border strips.
Cut nine 2½" (6.5 cm) sashing strips; cut two strips into six 12½" (31.8 cm) lengths.
Cut six 2½" (6.5 cm) binding strips.
See cutting directions for individual blocks for remaining directions

Assembling the Quilt

1. **Stitch** one block in each of the following patterns:
- Rail Fence block (page 66), using fabrics A, B, C, and D.
- Eight-pointed Star block (pages 69 to 71), using fabrics A and B.
- Nine-patch block (page 56), using fabrics A and E.
- Drunkard's Path block (pages 74 to 75), using fabrics A and B.
- Log Cabin block (page 61), using fabrics A, B, C, F, and G.
- Streak O' Lightning block (page 59), using fabrics A and B.
- Pinwheel block (page 67), using fabrics A and F.
- Double Nine-patch block (page 57), using fabrics A and B.
- Flying Geese block (pages 64 to 65), using fabrics A, C, and E.

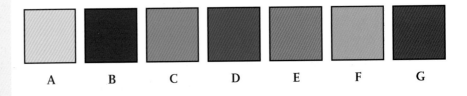

A B C D E F G

2. **Complete** quilt following General Directions, above; quilt, using stitch-in-the-ditch method.

How to Make Four Nine-patch and Double Nine-patch Pillows

(Shown on pages 10 and 53.) Finished sizes: 12" (30.5 cm); one block was used for each pillow.

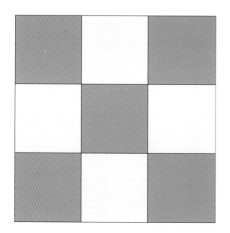 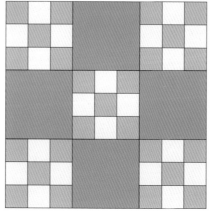

YOU WILL NEED

⅓ yd. (0.32 m) large print, for blocks.

¼ yd. (0.25 m) medium print, for blocks.

¼ yd. (0.25 m) small print, for blocks.

1 yd. (0.95 m) solid fabric, for blocks and ruffles.

½ yd. (0.5 m) grid print, for blocks and piping.

⅓ yd. (0.32 m) striped print, for piping.

Muslin, four 13" (33 cm) squares, for bottom quilt layer.

Batting, four 13" (33 cm) squares.

2¾ yd. (2.55 m) cording, ⁵⁄₃₂" (3.8 mm) diameter.

¾ yd. (0.7 m) fabric, for pillow backs.

16" (40.5 cm) hook and loop tape, ¾" (2 cm) wide, for back closures.

Four 12" (30.5 cm) pillow forms.

Cutting Directions

Cut 31 4½" (11.5 cm) squares (page 54);
    cut eleven from two large print strips,
    cut nine from one medium print strip,
    cut four from one small print strip,
    cut seven from one solid strip.

Cut two scant 1⅞" (4.7 cm) strips from each of the grid and solid fabrics.
Cut four 5½" (14 cm) ruffle strips.
Cut 1½" (3.8 cm) bias strips to cover cording.
Cut eight 12" × 9" (30.5 × 23 cm) rectangles, two for each pillow back.

Assembling the Pillows

1. Stitch three Nine-patch blocks (page 56), using solid with large print squares and medium with small print squares. Arrange squares as shown.

2. Stitch one Double Nine-patch block (page 57), using solid and grid squares with medium print squares.

3. Follow General Directions (opposite, steps 4 to 6); use stitch-in-the-ditch, grid, outline, and motif quilting techniques.

4. Stitch scant ¼" (6 mm) from outer edges of pillow tops. Trim batting and muslin even with sides. To make ruffles, stitch ends of two ruffle strips together; press in half. Gather raw edges together; pin to outer edges of pillow top, distributing gathers evenly. Stitch scant ¼" (6 mm) from edges. To add piping, wrap cord with bias strip; stitch, using zipper foot. Stitch piping to pillow top scant ¼" (6 mm) from edges, lapping ends.

5. Stitch 1" (2.5 cm) double-fold hem on one long edge of two rectangles, for each pillow back. Edgestitch 4" (10 cm) of hook tape to underside of one hem; edgestitch loop tape to top side of other hem.

6. Overlap back rectangles 1" (2.5 cm) at hemmed edges; baste. Trim pillow back to same size as quilted top, right sides together. Stitch ¼" (6 mm) seam allowance all around. Trim corners diagonally. Turn pillow cover right side out; press lightly. Insert pillow form.

How to Make a Double Nine-patch Table Topper

(Shown on page 53.) Finished size: 44" (112 cm) square.

YOU WILL NEED

2⅛ yd. (1.95 m) light fabric, for blocks, squares, and outer borders.

1⅛ yd. (1.05 m) dark fabric, for blocks, inner borders, and binding.

1⅓ yd. (1.27 m) fabric, for backing.

Batting, 48" (122 cm) square.

Cutting Directions

Cut 20 4½" (11.5 cm) light fabric squares (page 54) from three strips.
Cut four 12½" (31.8 cm) light fabric squares.
Cut seven light fabric strips and eight dark fabric strips a scant 1⅞" (4.7 cm) wide.
Cut four 1½" (3.8 cm) inner border strips.
Cut five 3½" (9 cm) outer border strips.
Cut five 2½" (6.5 cm) binding strips.

Assembling the Table Topper

1. Stitch five Double Nine-patch blocks (page 57).

2. Stitch the blocks to the light squares to make a large Nine-patch.

3. Complete table topper following General Directions (page 132, steps 3 to 7); use stitch-in-the-ditch, grid, motif, echo, and stipple quilting techniques.

How to Make a Rail Fence Lap Quilt

(Shown on page 50.) Finished size: 45" × 57" (115 × 144.5 cm); twelve 12" (30.5 cm) blocks are used.

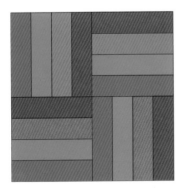

YOU WILL NEED

½ yd. (0.5 m) each of two fabrics, for blocks.

⅞ yd. (0.8 m) fabric, for blocks and inner border.

1½ yd. (1.4 m) fabric, for blocks, outer border, and binding.

1¾ yd. (1.6 m) fabric, for backing.

Batting, 49" × 61" (125 × 155 cm).

Cutting Directions

Cut eight 2" (5 cm) strips from each of four block fabrics.
Cut five 2" (5 cm) inner border strips.
Cut five 3½" (9 cm) outer border strips.
Cut six 2½" (6.5 cm) binding strips.

Assembling the Quilt

1. Stitch 48 Rail Fence squares (page 60).

2. Complete quilt following General Directions (page 132); stitch eight rows of six squares, arranged as shown, and quilt, using stitch-in-the-ditch method.

How to Make a Log Cabin Wall Hanging

(Shown on page 58.) Finished size: 56" (142 cm) square; sixteen 12¼" (31.2 cm) blocks are used.

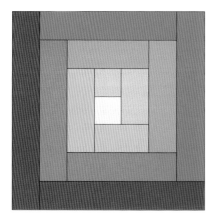

YOU WILL NEED

⅛ yd. (0.15 m) fabric A, for center square of block.

¼ yd. (0.25 m) fabric B.

⅜ yd. (0.35 m) fabric C.

½ yd. (0.5 m) fabric D.

⅝ yd. (0.6 m) fabric E.

¾ yd. (0.7 m) fabric F.

⅞ yd. (0.8 m) fabric G.

1¼ yd. (1.15 m) fabric, for border and binding.

2½ yd. (2.3 m) fabric, for backing.

Batting, 60" (152.5 cm) square.

⅓ yd. (0.32 m) muslin, for fabric sleeve.

Wood lath, 55" (139.5 cm) long.

Cutting Directions

Cut 2¼" (6 cm) strips from each fabric;
   cut one strip of fabric A; cut sixteen squares (page 54),
   cut three strips of fabric B,
   cut five strips of fabric C,
   cut seven strips of fabric D,
   cut eight strips of fabric E,
   cut ten strips of fabric F,
   cut twelve strips of fabric G.

Cut six 4" (10 cm) border strips.
Cut six 2½" (6.5 cm) binding strips.
Cut backing as necessary for a 60" (152.5 cm) square.

Assembling the Wall Hanging

1. Stitch sixteen Log Cabin blocks (page 61, steps 2 to 5); chainstitch (page 51) as much as possible. For example, chainstitch all center squares onto strip B, cut and press; chainstitch A/B units to strip B, chainstitch A/B/B units to strip C.

2. Complete wall hanging following General Directions (page 132); quilt, using stitch-in-the-ditch method.

3. Secure fabric sleeve (page 129) to quilt back.

How to Make a Flying Geese Pillow

(Shown on page 62.)

Cutting Directions

Cut pieces for one Flying Geese block as on page 64.
Cut two 5½" (14 cm) ruffle strips.
Cut two 12" × 9" (30.5 × 23 cm) rectangles for pillow backs.

Assembling the Pillow

1. Stitch one 12" Flying Geese block (pages 64 to 65).

2. Follow General Directions (page 132, steps 5 and 6); use stitch-in-the-ditch quilting method.

3. Complete pillow as on page 133, steps 4 to 6, adding gathered eyelet trim before attaching ruffle.

YOU WILL NEED

¾ yd. (0.7 m) fabric, for geese and ruffle.

⅛ yd. (0.15 m) fabric, for background.

⅜ yd. (0.35 m) fabric, for sashing and pillow back.

4" (10 cm) hook and loop tape, ¾" (2 cm) wide.

12" (30.5 cm) pillow form.

1½ yd. (1.4 m) pregathered eyelet trim.

How to Make a Flying Geese Lap Quilt

(Shown on page 62.) Finished size: 40" × 54" (102 × 137 cm); fifteen sets of seven geese are used.

Cutting Directions

Cut four 5¼" (13.2 cm) squares (page 54) from each goose fabric; cut squares diagonally in each direction (page 64).
Cut 105 squares from eight 2⅞" (7.2 cm) background strips; cut squares once diagonally.
Cut eight 2½" (6.5 cm) sashing strips.
Cut five 4½" (11.5 cm) border strips.
Cut five 2½" (6.5 cm) binding strips.

YOU WILL NEED

¼ yd. (0.25 m) each of seven fabrics, for geese.

¾ yd. (0.7 m) fabric, for background.

⅔ yd. (0.63 m) fabric, for sashing.

¾ yd. (0.7 m) fabric, for borders.

½ yd. (0.5 m) fabric, for binding.

Assembling the Lap Quilt

1. **Stitch** fifteen geese from each fabric, and stitch strips of seven geese (pages 64 and 65, steps 3 to 6), using each fabric in each strip.

2. **Stitch** three strips into one long strip; make five long strips (page 65, step 7).

3. **Complete** quilt following General Directions (page 132); stitch extra sashing strips as inner border strips. Quilt, using stitch-in-the-ditch method; freehand-quilt borders.

How to Make a Pinwheel Wall Hanging

(Shown on page 62.) Finished size: 32" (81.5 cm) square; four 12" (30.5 cm) blocks are used.

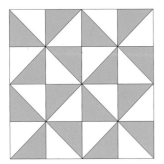

Cutting Directions

Cut eight 7¾" × 15½" (19.9 × 39.3 cm) rectangles;
cut two from each pinwheel fabric and four from background fabric.
Cut two 2½" (6.5 cm) sashing strips; cut two 12" (30.5 cm) lengths from one strip.
Cut four 3½" (9 cm) border strips.
Cut four 2" (5 cm) binding strips.

YOU WILL NEED

¼ yd. (0.25 m) each of two fabrics, for pinwheels.

½ yd. (0.5 m) fabric, for background.

⅞ yd. (0.8 m) fabric, for sashing, borders, and binding.

1 yd. (0.95 m) fabric, for backing.

Batting, 36" (91.5 cm) square.

⅓ yd. (0.32 m) muslin, for fabric sleeve.

Wood lath, 31" (78.5 cm) long.

Assembling the Wall Hanging

1. **Stitch** two pinwheel blocks from each fabric (page 67).

2. **Complete** wall hanging following General Directions (page 132); place identical blocks in opposite corners, and quilt, using stitch-in-the-ditch method.

3. **Secure** fabric sleeve (page 129) to quilt back.

How to Make an Eight-pointed Star Table Runner

(Shown on page 68.) Finished size: 12" × 60" (30.5 × 152.5 cm); five 12" (30.5 cm) blocks are used.

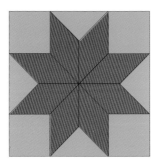

YOU WILL NEED

⅝ yd. (0.6 m) fabric, for stars and binding.

⅓ yd. (0.32 m) fabric, for stars.

½ yd. (0.5 m) fabric, for background.

¾ yd. (0.7 m) fabric, for backing.

Batting, 14" × 62" (35.5 × 157.5 cm).

Cutting Directions

Cut 20 diamonds (page 69) from each star fabric; use three 3" (7.5 cm) strips of each fabric.
Cut 20 squares (page 54) from two 4" (10 cm) background strips.
Cut 20 triangles (page 55) from five 6¼" (15.7 cm) background squares; cut squares diagonally in each direction.
Cut four 2" (5 cm) binding strips.

Assembling the Table Runner

1. Stitch five Eight-pointed Star blocks (pages 69 to 71).

2. Stitch blocks end to end, matching points.

3. Complete table runner following General Directions (page 132); quilt, using stitch-in-the-ditch method and echo technique.

How to Make an Eight-pointed Star Quilt

(Shown on pages 78 and 85.) Finished size: 37" (94 cm) square; sixteen 7¼" (18.7 cm) blocks are used.

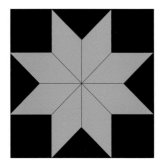

YOU WILL NEED

¼ yd. (0.25 m) each of four fabrics, for stars.

1¼ yd. (1.15 m) fabric, for background, borders, and binding.

½ yd. (0.5 m) contrasting fabric, for borders (may be one of first four fabrics).

1⅛ yd. (1.05 m) fabric, for backing.

Batting, 41" (104 cm) square.

Cutting Directions

Cut 32 diamonds (page 69) from each star fabric; use three 2" (5 cm) strips of each fabric.
Cut 64 squares (page 54) from five 2⅝" (6.8 cm) background strips.
Cut 64 triangles (page 63) from sixteen 4¼" (10.8 cm) background squares; cut squares diagonally in each direction.
Cut five 1¾" (4.5 cm) background border strips. Cut nine 1¾" (4.5 cm) contrast border strips.
Cut four 2½" (6.5 cm) binding strips.

Assembling the Quilt

1. Stitch sixteen Eight-pointed Star blocks (page 69).

2. Complete quilt following General Directions (page 132). In step 2, chainstitch rows (page 51), matching star points; stitch rows together, matching star points. In step 3, stitch border with interrupted corners (page 97). Quilt, using stitch-in-the-ditch method.

How to Make Two Drunkard's Path Placemats

(Shown on page 72.) Finished size: 12" × 18" (30.5 × 46 cm); 24 pieced squares are used in each.

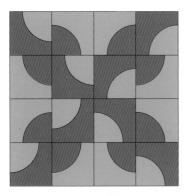

YOU WILL NEED

½ yd. (0.5 m) light fabric, for blocks.

¾ yd. (0.7 m) dark fabric, for blocks and binding.

½ yd. (0.5 m) fabric, for backing.

Two pieces of batting, 13" × 19" (33 × 48.5 cm) each.

Cutting Directions

Cut 36 3½" (9 cm) squares (page 54) from four light fabric strips; shape squares using large template (page 74).
Cut twelve 2½" (6.5 cm) squares from one light fabric strip; shape squares using small template.
Cut twelve 3½" (9 cm) squares and 36 2½"(6.5 cm) squares from dark fabric; shape squares as above.
Cut four 2" (5 cm) binding strips.

Assembling Two Placemats

1. Stitch twelve pieced squares with large dark pieces. Stitch 36 pieced squares with large light pieces.

2. Complete placemats following General Directions (page 132); quilt, using stitch-in-the-ditch method.

How to Make a Drunkard's Path Wall Hanging

(Shown on page 72.) Finished size: 41" (104 cm) square; nine 12" (30.5 cm) blocks are used.

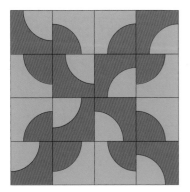

YOU WILL NEED

1⅓ yd. (1.23 m) light fabric, for blocks.

2 yd. (1.85 m) dark fabric, for blocks, borders, and binding.

1¼ yd. (1.15 m) fabric, for backing.

Batting, 44"(112 cm) square.

⅓ yd. (0.32 m) muslin, for fabric sleeve.

Wood lath, 40½" (103 cm) long.

Cutting Directions

Cut 72 3½" (9 cm) squares (page 54) from four light fabric strips; shape squares using large template (page 74). Repeat with dark fabric.
Cut 72 2½" (6.5 cm) squares from three light fabric strips; shape squares using small template. Repeat with dark fabric.
Cut four 3" (7.5 cm) border strips.
Cut four 2½" (6.5 cm) binding strips.

Assembling Two Placemats

1. Stitch nine Drunkard's Path blocks (page 74).

2. Complete quilt following General Directions (page 132); quilt, using stitch-in-the-ditch method.

3. Secure fabric sleeve (page 129) to quilt back.

How to Make an Ohio Star Flange Pillow

(Shown on page 80.) Finished size: 12" (30.5 cm) plus 2½" (6.5 cm) border flange.

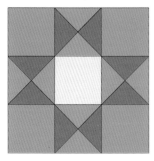

YOU WILL NEED

1 yd. (0.95 m) fabric, for block center, border flange, and pillow back.

⅜ yd. (0.35 m) each of two fabrics, for star points and background.

½ yd. (0.5 m) muslin, for backing.

4" (10 cm) of hook and loop tape, ¾" (2 cm) wide, for the closure.

Batting, about 22" (56 cm) square.

12" (30.5 cm) pillow form.

Cutting Directions

Cut squares and triangles for one Ohio Star block as on page 81.
Cut two 3" (7.5 cm) strips, for border.
Cut two 12" × 19" (30.5 × 48.5 cm) rectangles for pillow back.

Assembling the Pillow

1. Stitch one Ohio Star block (pages 81 to 82).

2. Complete pillow top following General Directions (page 132, steps 3 to 6); quilt, using stitch-in-the-ditch method.

3. Complete pillow as on page 133, steps 4 to 6. Before inserting pillow form, stitch in the ditch between the block and the border through all thicknesses, forming the flange.

How to Make an Ohio Star Quilt

(Shown on page 90.) Finished size: 33" (84 cm) square; sixteen 6" (15 cm) blocks are used.

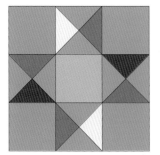

YOU WILL NEED

¼ yd. (0.25 m) fabric, for block center.

¼ yd. (0.25 m) each of four fabrics, for star points and sashing squares.

⅞ yd. (0.8 m) fabric, for block background and binding.

¼ yd. (0.25 m) fabric, for sashing strips.

½ yd. (0.5 m) fabric, for borders.

1 yd. (0.95 m) fabric, for backing.

Batting, about 37" (94 cm) square.

Cutting Directions

Cut sixteen 2½" (6.5 cm) squares (page 54) for block centers.
Cut eight 3¼" (8.2 cm) squares from each of four star point fabrics; cut these squares diagonally in both directions to make 32 triangles (page 64) of each fabric.
Cut 32 3¼" (8.2 cm) squares from three strips of background fabric; cut diagonally in both directions.
Cut 64 2½" (6.5 cm) squares from four background strips.
Cut nine 1½" (3.8 cm) connecting squares from one of the star point fabrics.
Cut four 1½" (3.8 cm) sashing strips; cut into 24 6½" (16.3 cm) lengths.
Cut four 3½" (9 cm) border strips.
Cut four 2" (5 cm) binding strips.

Assembling the Quilt

1. Stitch sixteen Ohio Star blocks (pages 81 to 82).

2. Complete quilt following General Directions (page 132). In step 2, stitch sashing strips with connecting squares between the blocks (page 93, steps 2 to 5). In step 3, stitch mitered borders to quilt top (page 96). Quilt, using stitch-in-the-ditch method; quilt border, using machine-guided or freehand techniques as desired.

How to Make a Churn Dash Table Topper

(Shown on page 90.) Finished size: 34" (86.5 cm) square; nine 6" (15 cm) blocks are used.

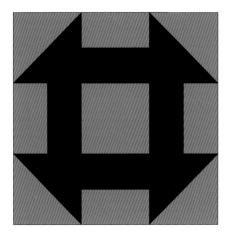

Cutting Directions

Cut 18 2⅞" (7.2 cm) squares (page 54) from design fabric; cut squares diagonally in one direction to make 36 triangles (page 63).
Cut 36 1½" × 2½" (3.8 × 6.5 cm) rectangles from design fabric.
Cut 36 triangles and 36 rectangles, same size as above, from background fabrics.
Cut nine 2½" (6.5 cm) squares from background fabrics, for the plain centers.
Cut seven 2½" (6.5 cm) strips for sashing and first border; use one strip to cut six 2½" × 6½" (6.5 × 16.3 cm) sashing pieces.
Cut four 1½"(3.8 cm) second border strips.
Cut four 3½" (9 cm) third border strips.
Cut four 2½" (6.5 cm) binding strips.

YOU WILL NEED

⅝ yd. (0.6 m) fabric, for block design and second border.

¼ yd. (0.25 m) each of three background fabrics.

1⅓ yd. (1.27 m) fabric, for sashing, first and third borders, and binding.

1⅛ yd. (1.05 m) fabric, for backing.

Batting, about 38" (96.5 cm) square.

Assembling the Table Topper

1. Stitch nine Churn Dash blocks (page 83).

2. Complete quilt following General Directions (page 132). In step 3, use lapped border method. Quilt around blocks and borders, using stitch-in-the-ditch method; freehand-quilt sashing and borders.

How to Make a Churn Dash Bed Quilt

(Shown on page 80.)

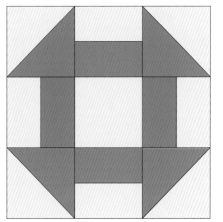

1. Cut and stitch Churn Dash blocks (page 83) following chart opposite. Stitch design and background strips before cutting 2½" (6.5 cm) squares; 280 for twin, 360 for full, 440 for queen.

2. Complete quilt following General Directions (page 132); in step 3, apply side borders first on twin and full-size quilt; use three strips for each queen-size side border.

3. Quilt, using stitch-in-the-ditch method.

	Twin	Full	Queen
Finished Size	62" × 86" (157.5 × 218.5 cm)	78" × 86" (198 × 218.5 cm)	86" × 93" (218.5 × 236.5 cm)
Drop length before quilting.	11" (28 cm) on three sides	12" (30.5 cm) on sides 11" (28 cm) on foot	13" (33 cm) on three sides
Number of 6" (15 cm) blocks; setting.	70 7 by 10	90 9 by 10	110 10 by 11

Adjust quilt size (page 30) for an extra-long bed or a longer drop length; consider sashing width if adding blocks.

	Twin	Full	Queen
You Will Need Fabric for block design.	2 yd. (1.85 m)	2⅜ yd (2.2 m)	2¾ yd. (2.55 m)
Three background fabrics.	⅞ yd. each (0.8 m)	1 yd. each (0.95 m)	1⅛ yd. each (1.05 m)
Fabric for sashing, border, binding.	3⅝ yd (3.35 m)	3¾ yd. (3.45 m)	4⅜ yd. (4 m)

(You will have extra block and background pieces when quilt is assembled.)

	Twin	Full	Queen
Cutting Directions Block design: cut into squares; cut into triangles.	10 140 280	13 180 360	16 220 440
1½" (3.8 cm) strips.	21	24	30
Each background fabric: 2⅞" (7.2 cm) strips; cut into squares; cut into triangles.	4 48 96	5 62 124	6 75 150
1½" (3.8 cm) strips.	7 24	8 31	10 38
2½" (6.5 cm) squares. Sashing: 2½" (6.5 cm) strips; 2½" × 6½" (6.5 × 16.3 cm) using rectangles.	24 60 10 strips	26 72 12 strips	30 90 15 strips
Border: 4½" (11.5 cm) strips.	8	8	10
Binding: 3" (7.5 cm) strips.	8	9	9

index